To my daughter
and all people – young and old –
who believe that our
contribution to making this world more
sustainable counts.

PETRA KUENKEL

MIND AND HEART

MAPPING YOUR PERSONAL JOURNEY
TOWARDS
LEADERSHIP FOR SUSTAINABILITY

Collective Leadership Institute
Building competence for sustainability

The German Library's bibliographical information: The German Library has recorded this publication in the German National Library's catalogue; detailed information can be accessed via http://dnb.ddb.de

Kuenkel, Petra
Mind and Heart – Mapping Your Personal Journey Towards Leadership for Sustainability
Copyright © 2008 Petra Kuenkel

Publishing and production: Books on Demand GmbH, Norderstedt, Germany.
Editing: Angela du Preez, Cape Town
Book layout and setting: buchgestaltung.de

A publication of the Collective Leadership Institute
www.collectiveleadership.com

All rights reserved.
No Portion of this work may be reproduced in any form or by any means, electronic, mechanical, photocopying, recording, or otherwise, without the written permission of the publisher.

ISBN-13: 978-3-8370-2799-0

CONTENTS

ABSTRACT
7

ACKNOWLEDGEMENTS
9

INTRODUCTION
11

CHAPTER ONE
UNFOLDMENT
23

CHAPTER TWO
PARTICIPATION
61

CHAPTER THREE
COHERENCE
95

CHAPTER FOUR
AWARENESS
131

CHAPTER FIVE
CONTRIBUTION
165

CHAPTER SIX
SUSTAINABILITY
203

BIBLIOGRAPHY
243

ILLUSTRATION OF MODELS
246

This book shows how leaders can use life and leadership experience to make a more meaningful contribution to the world.

ABSTRACT

What if we all knew the place within that is at home with the universe? What if we all knew how it feels to tend the common, the very force that nurtures all of us? This book leads us into the inner world of leadership that we often tend to deny: the intuitive insight – called initial deeper intention – that at the core of our leadership journey is our contribution to the collective evolutionary process. It matters what we do and how we think. The leadership journey, in this view, is a process of unearthing one's true nature in a spiralling movement, a growing self-expression in a gesture of responsiveness to what needs doing in the world.

Building on her own leadership journey and intensive conversations with 14 leaders from eight different countries around the world, Petra Kuenkel shows us how we can reconnect with the deeper theme of our journey and develop our own humanity as a gateway to world-consciousness. In this process lies a promise: the concern for the future of humanity is a consequence of cultivating one's own humanity. In a globalized and yet endangered world, the individual's insight and the world's enlightenment are intrinsically linked.

ACKNOWLEDGEMENTS

A book like this takes shape long before the first word is written. It begins even before the idea is born. Events happen, insights mature, encounters develop and life teaches unexpected lessons. Above all, writing is a creative act that involves the thoughts, words and actions of many people. All of these things are mixed in a sea of consciousness, out of which the writer selects what makes most sense to her. This book is a product of encounters over time with people, thoughts and events. Of all those who have helped to shape this book, I can only name those who contributed directly and those of whom I have become aware as indirect contributors.

For me, the wealth of this book lies in the many conversations I have had with leaders. In particular, I want to thank Tina Orlando, Dorian Baroni, Lechesa Tsenoli, Ayalew Zegeye, Nancy Clay, Marianne Isaakson, Gilles Desorbay, Elke Geising, Murray Low, Ahmed Ashaibani, Milda Zinkus, Martha Morris-Graham, Wayne Bush and Tom Robison for sharing their insights with me.

I am grateful to Peter Garrett for the insights into the deeper structures of life that have inspired the chapters of this book, and for his unshakeable belief in dialogue and inquiry. His library encouraged me to journey deeper into the literature of consciousness. I am grateful, too, to Bill Isaacs, for giving me the opportunity to learn about leadership and the role of dialogue. Thanks also to Beth Jandernoa and Glennifer Gillespie for their open support of women leaders.

I want to thank Christine Nachmann, Ryan Lemmer, Dave Bond and Kristiane Schäfer for their active support and encouragement; Robert Cran for the inspiring thoughts, and Vipassana for the practice of meditation that gave me practical insight into the development of consciousness.

INTRODUCTION

In the early 1960s, a girl grew up in the West of the divided city of Berlin. She lived with her parents in a beautiful area near the river from which she could, at times, hear shooting from the border – East German soldiers trying to prevent people from escaping the communist system. As a child, full of dreams, she battled with this reality. She never quite believed it, although each time her parents took the road along the terrifying fenced border, she almost stopped breathing for the ten frightening minutes it took to travel from her village to the big streets of the city. At the age of eight, she saw in a repeated daydream how all people, including East Germans and West Germans, took each other by the hand and walked over the border. And she saw how nothing terrible happened once this border was crossed. Rather, people celebrated peace, and the girl saw herself giving speeches about the possibility of all people living in harmony.

Some parts of her daydreams came true. I call this faculty of dreaming the initial deeper intention: the intuitive, half-rational, half non-rational feeling or insight, during childhood or adolescence, that the world *can* be a different place. It is an unconscious response to a call that is deeper than surface reality. It is almost a knowing that comes from a timeless place, a place that contains the eternal potential for humanity's reconciliation. If only we all nurtured our initial deeper intention. But the world outside us does not favour this inner knowing. Rather, the world often ignores it and educates it away.

When I became an adult, I remembered the story of my daydream when I began to talk with leaders about their young leadership stories. Only then did I realize the immense role of this earlier intention. For others, too, there was at least a trace of a memory of wanting to change the world or of wanting to be a force for good.

In ways that were not always conscious or consistent, this knowledge informed the professions I chose and the path my life took. It became an often-silent thread throughout my life and career. It was lost, found, then lost again, until it finally made its way back into mind and heart.

What if we all knew this place, the place within that is at home with the universe? What if we all knew how it feels to tend the common, and, in so doing, to nurture the very force that nurtures all of us? This book invites you on a journey into the inner world of leadership that we often ignore: the intuitive insight that, at the core of our leadership endeavour, is our contribution to the collective evolutionary process, a contribution to the sustainability of our world. *It matters what we do and how we think.* The personal leadership journey, in this view, is a process of unearthing our true nature, a growing self-expression that responds to what needs doing in the world.

The Berlin Wall fell because an uncounted number of people did what needed doing. With all shortcomings acknowledged, this was one of the moments in history when peaceful collective action changed the world.

Between the girl's daydream and the writing of this book lie years, journeys, experiences, aspirations, dreams and disappointments. But the core theme – the healing of fragmentation – has persistently presented itself to me as a call to action, no matter which form it took. It could not be silenced, not even in the most demanding of careers. I never consciously heeded the call. But it must have been at the centre of my decision to study medicine (a disappointing experience, because I found no healing of fragmentation in Western medicine). It must have been there when I attempted to understand people and the world by studying psychology and political science, in my frustration with traditionally fragmented Western science, in the insights I gained from my work in Africa, and finally in my work in leadership development and change management for sustainability.

INTRODUCTION

I was not always aware of the fact that the theme of my journey kept re-emerging. But it did, in questions, crises, contentment. It was only when I began to look at other people's journeys more consciously that I saw my own, reflected in their endeavours to realize not only their own potential as leaders, but also in their unique paths based on dreams, insights, revelations and authentic values. I realized that I was not the only one journeying on this path and not the only one with a leadership model that was constantly under construction. I began to see leadership journeys in a different light and thought there was something to be discovered about the initial deeper intention, the internal development of consciousness in individual leaders, and the impact this has on the world outside. I became interested in understanding leaders' concerns about making a wider contribution to the world. I decided to embark on a more structured inquiry into leadership journeys and their potential role as a gateway to increasing world-consciousness and more responsible business action.

But why leadership journeys, rather than ordinary life journeys? Because I do not see leadership as being separate from the rest of one's life. I believe that, because of their formal or emotional position of power, leaders influence the course of reality decisively. So their states of mind have an impact that is, conceivably, greater than others'. Leaders have raised their voices or have been given the authority to speak, and they influence reality because of this. Sometimes the mere fact that leaders hold positions of power makes them nodes in a larger network – and sometimes it is their resonance with others that places them there. The way they connect and communicate affects other people. No matter how conscious they are of this, a leader's actions are highly visible to others. Their behaviour affects areas beyond the obvious, areas often found beyond their official tasks. I therefore assume that leaders, regardless of their official capacity, have a special obligation, an almost undeniable responsibility – they need to become conscious of how they influence reality.

I see the leadership journey as a process of unfolding consciousness in response to one's impact on the world. It is a growing expression of a person's individuality, gifts and experienced-based wisdom that leads to an increasing awareness of what needs doing. This usually develops in a domain of influence that goes beyond the private sphere, and includes a relational position of power. In my view, the leadership journey holds, at its core, the deeper initial intention – and its underlying theme is uncovering a deep-rooted concern for humanity through becoming aware of one's own humanity. This, in turn, creates authentic value and has a potentially positive impact – on the world, for other people, for humankind. It is the cornerstone for *leadership for sustainability*.

The process of unfolding towards greater awareness of one's true responsibility in the world is the thread that runs through this book. The significance of this process is clearly evident when seen against the backdrop of the evolution of human consciousness.

Despite the fact that the world is hugely fragmented, that the problems causing war and poverty are far from being solved, and that disparity and an endangered environment are the order of the day, there is also a slow but growing movement towards a more sustainable world. From all walks of life, from business, civil society, governments, spiritual communities and committed individuals, comes a sincere attempt to put the future of humankind and of this planet on the agenda and to keep it there. Often fragmented, sometimes in competition, at times with little real effect, the call for change is becoming noticeably stronger. Despite the still-widespread feeling of powerlessness regarding the course the world takes with all its suffering and atrocities, consciousness seems to be changing and gradual changes in concern and responsibility are being brought to, or forced into, the world of business.

INTRODUCTION

It is likely that the kind of leadership in international businesses today will decisively influence how the world develops. It would seem, then, that big business, more than any other factor, will determine the world's course, and, therefore, the future of humankind.

But every change in an organization results from the choices made by dedicated people. Leaders who examine their lives, their choices, and their values can begin to experience themselves as co-creators of an interconnected reality. There is hope that the leadership in global as well as local organizations will respond, out of a sense of interconnectedness and co-responsibility, to questions about human dignity, inclusiveness, and fairer distribution of wealth. It might finally respond to the call for a sustainable world. However, since every business, every organization is made up of individuals, there is very little chance of a change in consciousness unless the change also takes place within each individual.

The collectively expressed need for sustainable action surely supports the inner process of accessing one's own potential to contribute to humanity. But the process remains particular to each leader, and neither its form nor its timing can be predicted. The road to humanity is different for each leader – there are no shortcuts or recipes. I believe that accessing one's own humanity is crucial to the development of world consciousness and to a deeper compassion for the world.

From the many encounters I have had with leaders from various parts of the world, I have noticed a remarkable aspect of today's reality: the desire to make a difference is present in many leaders, however deeply buried. I met very, very few who, if sincerely questioned, would not find deep in their heart the aspiration to contribute to a better world.

Beneath the surface, there is an unexpressed need to create more meaning, more connectedness, and more relatedness, and to help improve the lives of others. Wanting to make a difference in the world by serving humankind is probably the most widely suppressed desire in organizations and among leaders. A senior manager from a multinational company phrased it like this:

> *What I feel is that every person actually has a core that wants to serve ... and it is more about uncovering it, because this gets silenced, cut off, nobody is asking for it, nobody is rewarding it in the organization. You almost have to do it against all odds.*

This latent desire is what I would like to encourage you to rediscover, explore and cultivate. If you don't do it, nobody will do it for you. And the world's course depends on each person's contribution.

If my assumption is correct, if, at the bottom of a leader's aspiration, is the desire to serve the world, accessing such aspiration cannot only free you to follow your authentic self, it will also open the way to more responsible and responsive leadership. The change out there in the world cannot be separated from the change inside you. Issues of sustainability need a response from each person's heart, or they won't be sustainable. At the same time, the personal development of leaders needs to reflect more than effectiveness and performance. It needs to become a pathway to sustainable future action in this world. Inspired by one another, mind and heart will develop in unison.

In 2003 I encountered a book in a little bookstore in Bombay, India. There on the shelf was a booklet made of inexpensive material entitled *The Future of Humanity*. It was a book documenting a dialogue between two people that took place twenty years earlier – the Western physicist David Bohm and the Eastern metaphysician J. Krishnamurti. The conversation centred on the fact that the contributions of modern science and technology never seemed to be used for the greater good of humanity. In the end, they were always used for destruction, and that this had its origins in the distorted mental activity that formed the basis of human behaviour and not in the technology itself (Krishnamurti & Bohm, 1986).

Krishnamurti's base assumption is that human thought creates divisions – between 'me' and 'you' and between 'me' and 'the world'. It then acts on these divisions as if they were facts. To nobody's surprise, the mental activity that continues to fragment shows up as polarization in the world: difference, disparity and conflict. The way Krishnamurti saw it, we all live in a world of illusion, thinking that 'my' consciousness is different from another person's consciousness, and, in doing so, we constantly recreate the illusion of separation we see in the world. In the booklet David Bohm poses a crucial question: 'Do you want to say there is *one* consciousness of mankind?' (Krishnamurti & Bohm, 1986, p. 24) and Krishnamurti responds in his straightforward way: 'It is all one.'(ibid.). For him, at the core of the human condition is the illusion of separation, in which each person struggles alone, trying to fulfil himself or herself to achieve peace, happiness and security. And yet, if consciousness is all one, no one can win the struggle for fulfilment in isolation.

The very attempt to separate one's own happiness from the suffering of others would be a reinforcing activity that would maintain separation and create more suffering, more disparity and more conflict. Hence, only the understanding, or, rather, the experience, of reality as being composed of *one* consciousness of humankind can pave the way for the liberation of the human mind. The transformation of human thought would require overcoming the illusion of separation, individually and collectively. For Krishnamurti, only this radical transformation of thought patterns could effect real change in the world. For him, the future of humanity depends on this transformation of the human mind (Krishnamurti & Bohm, 1986). And he is convinced that a different collective outcome is only possible if this process takes place within the individual.

This particularly radical view inspired me to explore my own and other leaders' journeys in terms of their interaction with memory, thought, insight, transcendence of experience, and bringing forth enactment of reality. That humble little booklet had posed a challenge to my busy consultancy work in the world: that the transformation of collective thought patterns towards sustainable action in the world is highly dependent on the authentic transformation of the individual mind. This is why the inner transformative process of leaders is the starting point for my writing. My base assumption is that in the process of *bringing oneself into the world*, the increasingly authentic self-expression of a leader is inextricably linked to and influenced by human consciousness as a whole. And vice versa – the development of consciousness within the individual has an influence on human consciousness as a whole. Thus, in terms of human consciousness, it does matter what leaders think and how they evolve internally. The world, if I adopt the thinking of Krishnamurti, is co-created by consciousness, by collective and individual thought, and only subsequently by action. Thus, more conscious participation by leaders in the movement towards the regeneration and sustainability of life on this planet could engender hope for the future of humanity.

Based on my own leadership journey and on extensive conversations with 14 leaders from eight different countries, this book invites you to reconnect with the deeper theme of your journey and to develop your own humanity as a gateway to world-consciousness and leadership for sustainability. The leaders I spoke with came from various cultures: American, European, Arabic, African. They were of different ages (28 to 58); male and female; and they held different leadership positions in multinational companies, governments, unions, NGOs and their own small companies. All of them had begun to ask questions regarding their leadership contribution, the kinds of questions that do not have ready answers, great stories or wise speeches, but were worth pondering for a while. What started out as a three-month enquiry ended up taking six to nine months in most cases. In the various conversations, patterns of thought and experience became evident and insights emerged in partial response to the question: What prompts us to access our humanity on a deeper level and subsequently to become more concerned about humanity as a whole? The key to understanding our leadership role could not be found on the surface by looking at our activities and tasks. Below the surface, we found an inner world with a leadership model constantly under construction in response to inner experiences and outside events. This deeper source within, that nurtures and informs the way in which we collectively bring forth a world, is essential for the journey. Leading can take place anywhere, from within or outside an organization, and from different levels of the organization's hierarchy. Positional power and roles of leadership can change, but the journey of leading from within continues.

Both the struggles and achievements of leaders count. It is the way in which we try to make sense of our path towards maturity that becomes the essence of our journey. Inspired by Krishnamurti's suggestion that consciousness is *one* (Krishnamurti, 1978), I realized that when we acknowledge, support and understand the maturing awareness of one another, we begin to glimpse the whole of consciousness. As awareness expands, so the desire to contribute grows. Leading from a deeper place within values the individual, while encompassing the interests of the collective and of the greater good. This book assumes that the very inner quality of leadership, the expression of one's particular voice, is, in its deepest essence, always based on an intention to favour life. Providing leadership that is in tune with the greater good is a quality available to all people. Leading consciously and for the benefit of humanity is not about gaining yet another set of skills, acquiring more interpersonal capabilities, or adding a new leadership strategy to our repertoire; rather, it is a process of dropping a load, of peeling off the layers of memory and expectation, of freeing oneself from the demands of normative behaviour, and of finding home, of unearthing what is, and always has been, there. Only then do we feel closest to the Universe, to others, and to ourselves, and can lead from an inner centre that is not fragmented, not separated from the world 'out there'. In this state of heart and mind, acting in a way that benefits the world and humanity seems less ambitious, less demanding. It seems to be the natural way. Compassion becomes a constant companion, and so does the desire to contribute. There is lightness about leading more consciously, even though it is often gained through hard experience. There are helpful skills, things one can learn, discover, or acquire on the road to more conscious leadership, but none of these ingredients are a substitute for the personal transformative process we experience in its particular form, shape and sequence. The essence of our leadership journey is about growing into our true identity as a leader and, by doing so, accessing an intelligence that is greater than ourselves and encompasses the whole. In a globalized yet endangered world, our individual insight and the world's enlightenment are intrinsically linked.

This book invites you to review your own leadership journey in the light of other people's experiences. It offers you the stories, thoughts and insights of fellow travellers that can inspire, console or encourage you. It will also offer you passages of theory that might help to relate insights to recent or timeless scientific thought, as well as suggestions for further reading. You can choose to ignore the theory – it will be clearly marked! There is a summary at the end of each chapter and a passage for reflection. My advice: do not answer the questions diligently. Take them with you, on a plane, into the next stressful meeting, on a holiday. Just carry them around so that they pop up in your mind every now and then. If you wish, take notes. But do not force yourself. Let the process be organic rather than structured, and the questions might just trigger questions of your own.

Questions are there to transform the mind. Or as Rainer Maria Rilke said in his 'Letters to a Young Poet':

> I want to beg you, as much as I can, to be patient toward all that is unresolved in your heart and try to love the questions themselves like locked rooms and like books that are written in a very foreign tongue. Do not seek the answers, which cannot be given to you because you would not be able to live them. And the point is to live everything. Live the questions now. Perhaps you will then, gradually, without noticing it, live along some distant day into the answers.

INTRODUCTION

Reflections

If you see your life as a journey with places you have been and places you might still go to, where do you think you are at this moment?

What is the question that is currently uppermost in your mind?

If you had no security or money constraints, what would you most like to do?

CHAPTER ONE
UNFOLDMENT

I do not know where this book found you – in an airport bookstore just before embarking on a business trip, at your favourite holiday resort, on the shelf next to your bed in winter time, or among your birthday presents. Lives are different and so are leadership journeys. But I do know that if you're reading this book, a question is taking form in your mind or in the mind of someone close to you. It may not be well formulated, it may be vague, reluctant to be expressed, or it may have been hammering in your mind loudly enough to stop ignoring it. You might feel lonely at times with this question and experience increasing alienation, as if you were the only one who thinks or feels like this, the only one who does not feel entirely at home in this world. Or it may be less than the seed of a question; it may simply be a vague feeling of tiredness, a fear of insignificance, a hurtful absence of meaning in your life, a feeling of being lost, an inner numbness, or a palpable sense of rising emptiness. Or you might have picked up this book because it resonated with you, because it expressed the feelings you have had for some time.

Maybe this book has found you in the middle of a real crisis, in an experience of loss or disappointment, in the wake of a change that you did not initiate, or in a time when you feel undeniably stuck. Or maybe you're content with the achievements in your life, but you sense faint anxiety because you suspect they may not last.

There are innumerable ways in which the human mind and heart prompt us to pay attention and to ask ourselves where to go from here. And there are as many ways of ignoring the cues. Whether you're paying attention or ignoring the cues, please consider simply observing. Just that: observe what is happening. You aren't the only one on this journey. There are many others travelling this path.

But it is *your* mind and *your* heart responding to something that is no longer lying dormant within you. It is a reminder that your leadership journey is a quest, that it always has been and always will be one. There is no guarantee that you'll ever reach the final destination – but there is a promise that the longer the journey is, the more you will have understood about the human mind and the human heart, and the nature of consciousness. There may never be an answer to the question of what exactly your contribution is, but, with a bit of luck, you may well come closer to a feeling of being at home in the Universe.

Not long after his dialogues with Krishnamurti, David Bohm developed his theory about the 'implicate and explicate order'. In a conversation with the leadership thinker Joe Jaworsky, he explains:

> Yourself is actually the whole of mankind. That's the idea of the implicate order – that everything is enfolded in everything. The entire past is enfolded in each of us in a subtle way. If you reach deeply into yourself, you are reaching into the very essence of mankind. When you do this, you will be led into the generating depth of consciousness that is common to the whole of mankind and that has the whole of mankind enfolded in it. The individual's ability to be sensitive to that becomes the key to the change of mankind. We are all connected. If this could be taught, and if people could understand it, we would have a different consciousness. (David Bohm, cited in Jaworsky. 1996, p. 80)

Whether you recognize it or not, there is an unfolding taking place through you in your leadership journey. It may not be entirely in your hands, but it is not happening without your permission either – you aren't passive in this process.

A Glimpse into Theory: David Bohm's Theory of the Implicate and Explicate Order

The quantum physicist David Bohm describes the order that underlies all visible order (understand: visible physical and mental structure), as the 'implicate order'. The implicate order (from Latin 'to be enfolded, to fold inward') is a level of reality that can be imagined as lying beyond our normal everyday thoughts and perceptions, and also beyond any of the models of reality offered by traditional scientific theory. What we see as well as what we construct mentally belongs to the 'explicate order' (Jaworsky, 1996, p. 78). In the implicate order, one could say that everything is *enfolded* into everything, invisibly, very much like Krishnamurti's concept of *one consciousness*. In this deeper order of nature, everything is interwoven with everything else, forming the underlying source of what we see as manifest reality – the explicate order, where things are physically or mentally manifested. Each such manifested entity is perceived as existing in its own particular region of space (and time) and outside the regions belonging to other things (Bohm 1996, p. 177). Quantum physicists look below this surface reality into sub-atomic reality with its field of potentiality that gives rise to the physical world. What they find is only potential and constant change.

David Bohm believes that our organs of perception cause us to fall prey to an illusion, thinking that not only are the things we see and the thoughts we have separate from each other, they also seem to be all there is to reality. Buddhist philosophy is founded on a similar conclusion. Physical reality is called maya (illusion), which we believe is all there is, ignoring the vast underlying interconnected reality. Bohm suggests that if we became aware of the *oneness* of all things on a deeper level, including the oneness of all humankind, we would see that ill will, competition, hatred, violence, and conflict are nothing more than unconscious acts of self-destruction (Bohm, 1996).

Another quantum physicist, Dana Zohar, describes this underlying reality as a kind of undercurrent, almost like a vast sea (Zohar & Marshall, 1994, p. 331). As human beings we are like excitations, ripples on the surface of the quantum vacuum's sea of potentiality (ibid, p. 274). We are temporary yet relatively stable structures over a certain period of time, like temporary forms to be seen on a surface. Like everything else, we are part of nature's evolving reality. Life is a never-ending flux of enfoldment and unfoldment. Everything undergoes constant change. Even what we see as manifest and stable is constantly under reconstruction: we ourselves, mind and body, the world.

When you find yourself in any of the states I mentioned above, I believe it is worth looking at the early part of your journey. Your memory might be scattered or faint. It might take time to remember anything at all. But I am sure there were secret daydreams, fairy encounters, heroes you admired, books you were fascinated by, a painful experience that triggered a quest, a silent promise to yourself, dreams of discovery, visions of being a saviour, empathy with suffering, an identification with heroes who represent deeper human values. No two young leadership stories are the same. So don't expect grand visions. Look for the value beneath your memories, the emotionally charged insights. Take your time to unearth the ordinary details. Collect the scraps of memory patiently. Gradually begin to listen to your leadership journey, as if there were a connection to a great

CHAPTER ONE: UNFOLDMENT

underlying tune that is constantly playing yet so difficult for us to hear. While you begin to search your memory, listen to this.

In the early 1950s in rural Ethiopia, a boy named Samson had reached school-going age. He had grown up with a father he admired for his strong character:

> He never submitted to power and went every mileage after the truth. He loved human beings, irrespective of their social status, and he had a way of simply acknowledging your existence and giving the required space for whatever was there to exist.

His father proposed that he go to a modern school. But, at the age of seven, Samson violently opposed this – he refused to attend a modern school. Ethiopia was predominantly Orthodox Christian and for a long time, the traditional church had been the only source of education. At that time, modern schools were associated with non-orthodox Christian religion. Samson with his bright seven-year-old mind concluded that going to a modern school would mean that he would have to change his faith and convert to modern Catholicism. His father, a peasant in a traditional culture, could have forced the boy, but he did not. Samson says:

> He acknowledged me as an equal because I existed and I needed to be given the space I deserved. So what he did was to take me to the head of the Orthodox Church in our neighbourhood to convince me that going to a modern school would not mean I had to change my faith. This experience – to be treated like an equal by my father – was absolutely crucial for me. It lives with me and in me.

There it is – a strong and deep value, timeless, resiliently placed in

CHAPTER ONE: UNFOLDMENT

the collective human consciousness: the conviction that people are equal and should be treated as equals. Implicit in this conviction is an intuitive knowing that borders separate what belongs together; the insight that the world needs tolerance and enlightenment; the desire to experience and create harmony; an admiration for people who fight for justice; and a fascination with the diversity of the human race.

Children have innumerable ways of relating to eternal human values. Edith's parents lived in the country side in southern Germany. Her mother and father had a hard time. Edith's mother didn't come from the 'right' social class. Her father should not have married her and people made sure she was always aware of this. It was 1960 and Germany had not entirely recovered from the Second World War. At the age of 14, Edith began to escape into books and music: Beethoven and Simone de Beauvoir. She wrote in her diary:

> I have a dream to change the world. Tolerance, tolerance, tolerance. I want to be the most tolerant person, and enlightened, really have clarity, and really understand how the world functions. Equality, and respect, respect for the dignity of a human being, no matter what race or colour or religion.

This intention stayed with her and became a driving force throughout her life.

At the core of what I call the initial deeper intention is a perception of incoherence – the world is different from one's intuitive insight, it contradicts the deeper value one has experienced in insights, dreams, and admirations. Here the initial deeper intention develops: this has got to change. This needs healing. The world needs to become how it is meant to be. I want to understand how the world works. The intention is intuitively geared to healing, to contributing to life, to serving, to wanting to create change for the better. There is, at times, a frightening element of loneliness – the child or young adult senses that this deeper feeling of how things ought to be is not widely acknowledged. It might be better to keep it a secret, this stuff of dreams, diaries, and journeys of the mind. But even though it is buried, the intention has formed and it begins to form the mind in subtle ways.

How this happens depends on the mind and circumstances of the young person. And it is not always a conscious process. The pieces of the puzzle that you might be able to see in retrospect might have been there all along. There is no way of knowing how accessible this intention is to the growing mind of an adolescent, and no way of telling how it will influence choices and how resilient it will become. But I believe that many more people than we think are aware of the whole and have an intuitive feeling about what is needed in the world.

Lucia, the child of mixed Italian and English parentage, grew up in London. In the early 1980s, there was a TV series she loved very much. Her absolute super heroine was Wonder Woman.

> Wonder Woman was very cool, she was such a superhero and she would save whoever was in trouble. As soon as she was needed she pulled a lasso out of her belt and she would swing the lasso over her head and become Wonder Woman, the saviour.

In her dreams Lucia *was* Wonder Woman. At the age of 11, Lucia knew that she wanted to become a lawyer. She loved debates, she loved arguing, and she wanted to fight for the underdog. She wanted to help people who did not have a voice, who were condemned for the wrong reasons or who could not get themselves out of difficulties.

I believe that the initial intention is the starting point for your leadership journey. It is a resilient underlying theme, not necessarily

CHAPTER ONE: UNFOLDMENT

rational and seldom realistic, but nonetheless a deeply held emotional thread that informs your journey into adult life. For some people it grows into a clear vision for change in the outer world during adolescence, following a realization about what the world seems to need, and, subsequently, about what one needs to do in the world to help it to become a better place. For other people, it remains a vague underlying rhythm, masked by the experience of its irrelevance in the outer world. The intention too often gets lost in the turmoil of finding one's place in private and professional life – even the strongest of visions is sometimes dismantled by the impossibility of its implementation, and the intention is slowly buried by disappointments and disillusionments. But, somehow, it surfaces again in different guises throughout the journey until it makes itself known as questions that turn up at different points of the journey. This thread consciously or unconsciously informs the choice of profession, places, organizations, tasks.

During the years in which he grew, Samson's deeply held conviction about respect and dignity for each and every person in the world became an unconscious guiding force. Education and exposure to the world made him see that the value he so strongly internalized was not at all commonly applied. This triggered deeper questions in life. As a young adult, he wanted to know how the world works, so he plunged into philosophy and politics. The more he saw of the world, the more he knew that it did not operate according to his deeper values – neither the world at large nor Ethiopian society. He dreamt of changing his society, thinking that there must be a way of overcoming the misery and destitution. His bright mind gravitated to the revolutionary writings of Marx, Lenin and Mao. The warrior in him adopted the commitment to change and took on the Marxist resolve to struggle. He believed this was the only way of bringing about transformation. Samson joined the political party whose strategy was to fight for political power and thus to change society. But his dream got lost – the movement was crushed by the brutal force of Ethiopia's military dictatorship. Samson was imprisoned. He spent four years of his young life behind bars, in conditions that most of his fellow prisoners did not survive. Samson later said:

> Like any inexperienced young person, I used to believe that it is possible to change the world into what you want it to be. From the prison experience, I understood what power can do, what it can be used for, and that changing the world to your ideal is not such an easy task. I learned that social change requires something beyond wishes and desires.

A willingness to understand the world or to change it goes hand in hand with a growing need to participate in the world. If you care to look for it, the urge to create change, to bring forth the world, to express one's gift, to invent helpful things, underpins a young person's desire to understand the world and fascination with difference. Although it may differ in intensity, form and content, this urge fuels young people's excitement about moving forward in life, taking a stand, and taking the lead. This does not mean that it works the way we intend it to. The world does not want to be changed. People do not understand our intention. Others do not necessarily agree with our vision. Those we want to help do not want to be helped. Sometimes, what we choose to do, inspired by our intention, ends up failing to support our values.

Edith left the narrow-minded German countryside where life and the Catholic convent school kept forcing her to conform, and she set out to discover the world. Reading Simone de Beauvoir had opened up her mind to a different world, a world that was to be explored and changed. She stayed faithful to her deeper values and her desire to understand the human condition. She studied psychology and social work, only to confront the rigidity and conformity of academia when she became a member of a university faculty in Switzerland. Her dreams of a free and equal world still called her, and she went to New York to work in the Bronx. She says:

> I took my psychology into the black community in New York, and worked for seven years in Harlem in the Bronx. I discovered many things: I could organize, I could brand social services, but I could only do these things because I was accepted. And they accepted me certainly not because I was a psychologist or because I was white, or because I could organize, they accepted me because I accepted them, just that, the way they were, as equals.

I believe that the leadership journey begins long before we ever get the chance to move into an official leadership position. There is a perceptible search for coherence that is fuelled by the initial deeper intention. Both engender the beginnings of a quest, and are probably the most underestimated or neglected forces in a leadership journey. The quest contains the deeper values. For some, it becomes a set of very strong political or moral values; for others, it is transformed into passionate work or high achievement. It is influenced by education, politics, and experience. And it strengthens and weakens according to how the world receives – or rejects – its nature. The quest arises from, and is continually nourished by, a repeated return to the deeper core values. These are not the morally imposed values we internalize through religious exposure or by being in a particular political context; neither are they the values taught by society, parents, schools, higher education or organizational cultures.

A quest based on an early intention is nourished by a deeper ground of knowing. We have all experienced such knowing – through other people, nature, books that resonated with our hearts, movies that touched our souls. Nobody taught us. It did not reach us through the intellect. We knew it when we felt it. And we usually know when the quest gets lost, when it withers, when it fades.

Lucia went after her dream – she got a degree in law. She contemplated becoming a barrister, but could not afford it. After her time at the university she went to Italy to teach English. Through a friend she found a job at a very good law firm. But awakening to reality was frightening – the atmosphere in the law firm came straight out of a Charles Dickens novel, complete with old-fashioned structures. Happily, the owner of the law firm was impressed by her work and encouraged her to stay. He promised her that she would become a junior partner in two years and a senior partner in five. When Lucia saw this vision of her life mapped out in front of her, she left. The map bore no relation to her real quest. But she had learnt to listen to her inner voice and to risk change. It was not much different in the law firm she worked at in London – an atmosphere that dampened creativity, with very little real human contact, no room for change and no people to save. So her quest continued. There was truth in her quest. Her wish to make a contribution that would have a lasting impact, her old dream of changing the balance of power between the haves and the have-nots, was faint, but still alive. The fact that she had studied environment and energy law during her time at university made her search more consciously for a structure in which she could evolve and to which she could contribute at the same time. After thorough research she decided to join a multinational energy company.

The very pattern that sets the theme of the journey – the early intention, the experience of incoherence, the quest – sometimes unfolds into two parallel paths: the willingness to redress something 'out there' in the world, and the search for our own healing. The two paths cannot be separated. Each nurtures and inspires the other, and very often in healing others we heal ourselves. In creating

CHAPTER ONE: UNFOLDMENT

harmony for others, we create harmony for ourselves. In overcoming injustice, we might heal our own experiences of injustice. In helping people to find their voice, we may find our own voice. In this way, each leadership journey results in personal integration while it aids integration in the world. For some people, it is easy to trace what in themselves they needed to heal. For others, it is almost impossible to remember – the pain was so strong that memory deleted the experience. Whether or not you feel that you need healing, the quest is based on a search for inner and outer coherence.

As an adolescent, you might rarely, if ever, have thought about leading. And you could never have anticipated the long and winding road that was in front of you. But the longing for coherence, by whatever means, was there, and so was the desire to understand, to create, to take part: all the stuff that leadership journeys are made of. There might have been dreams you gave up on, or aspirations that turned out to be too ambitious. Or you did achieve what you wanted to, with pride. For most of us the desire to actively and creatively participate in our own and the world's unfolding is a driving force. I believe what gets lost all too often is the core of the underlying intention: the very essence that was meant to go beyond the actualization of yourself, the deeper dream that was meant to heal the world, or some piece of it. Long after the early intention has faded, long after the dream is lost, the quest for coherence continues, randomly, more superficially, and directed at the outer world. We hope to come home by changing the external environment, by trying to find a better match, a new relationship, a different job, companies, places, houses, countries, by overworking or breaking free from the world, by immersing ourselves in a hectic social life or by withdrawing from the world. And this will keep happening until the incoherence becomes so unbearable that we know something within needs to change. Whether forced or voluntary, reflection increases our ability to notice that no outer coherence will appear without at least a degree of inner coherence. We might get trapped in the constant search for coherence in the outer world and only if that fails, begin to start asking different kinds of questions. This might sound arduous. But it need not be.

The first door into your leadership journey opens when you begin to observe both the past and the present; when you begin to recollect your memory, gather the scattered pieces of what might have been your early intention, when you begin to feel there could have been a quest, the first door has opened.

The second door opens when you begin to accept. This is how I have come to be. As Bill Isaacs says, 'Ultimately, we perceive the coherence of the world as we extend forgiveness – to ourselves and others' (Isaacs, 1999, p. 69). Acceptance is the only road to compassion. This does not imply agreement or approval, just acceptance. This is how things have come to be. This is me in it. The experience of 'feeling at home in the universe', wholeheartedly acknowledging your existence, is probably the closest description I can give. Not every crisis leads to a phase of stillness, a halt and the openness to ask new questions. We have the desire to maintain our identity the way it is, we find immediate solutions, and this prevents, or outmaneuvers contemplation. This is perfectly all right. There is no need to read signs into every event in life. But if you feel that there is a deeper loss of orientation, a lasting question regarding what your contribution could be, a pervasive sadness that this might be all there is or a serious doubt about the direction of your path, it is worthwhile turning your ear to the wind and listening to a deeper song. There is one. When we feel we've run dry because of the never-ending busyness of life, and when a list of uncounted chores is placed between us and our hearts, then it is time to invite stillness. The outer world no longer aligns with our deeper values. Something that never had a chance to be heard before wants to be heard now.

CHAPTER ONE: UNFOLDMENT

Reconnecting with your early intention is a very important step in reclaiming the essence of your leadership quest. It involves asking your mind to create order in your memory. This is not always comfortable. You'll most probably come up against resistance: I cannot remember; there's nothing to remember. Never mind. There *is* a young leadership story, a context of experience in which your urge to create unfolded, in which deeper insights arose your heart. There were inspirations, discoveries, and turning points. There is a thread that leads to where you are now: choices, achievements, disappointments and more choices. Let the questions lead you, even if they change over time. Sometimes they might get lost in the hurried passage of daily events, or they may be violently silenced by reason. The purpose of questions is to clarify the inner search, not to find a quick solution to your current situation. If you want to reshape your leadership journey or redesign your contribution, you need creative space to reframe your current view of the world and your place in it. You need to enter the uneasy melting pot of inner transformation.

When you search your memory, you might find that your leadership journey does not have a marked beginning. A deeper underlying quest might have begun long before you ever came close to anything like an official leadership position. When you moved into a leadership position, you did not think of it as such, nobody really prepared you. You could not quite make out the difference. There might have been signposts along the way, showing you that there was always an underlying quest – a phase of hesitation, a period of uncertainty about what is right and what is wrong, a question that kept coming to mind, a dissatisfaction that you could not respond to on an outer level (and decided to ignore), or an experience that left you without explanation. A persistent question unanswered is always an invitation to inquiry, a reminder of the journey.

CHAPTER ONE: UNFOLDMENT

Like any other person, a leader goes through various cycles of learning. The path is rarely straightforward. It is more often a river meandering its way to the delta. But there are moments that signal significant change: the journey of life turns into a more conscious leadership journey. Suddenly your way of participating in life has changed. The more independent discovery phase of your adolescence gives way to a different pattern – you become more embedded in the societal and organizational system. You have assumed certain responsibilities in your profession and in your family. All of a sudden your word counts, your decisions have an impact beyond yourself and sometimes beyond your imagination; you carry a responsibility that, if not used mindfully, could damage others. People expect something of you. You are entering a whole net of expectations and demands that begin to shape your identity in a different way. Your early intention might have withered or still be alive, your deeper leadership journey might have begun long before, but now reality places its demands on your desk. You might feel you are not old enough to meet the demands. There is the thrill of challenge mixed with doubts about your capabilities and your willingness to operate in contexts you did not consciously choose. The world you enter does not necessarily promote or support your quest, and nobody asks for your deeper intention.

Lucia chose the multinational energy company as the setting for her quest, not entirely for career reasons. She wanted to be able to influence things in an environment where people count and where there was at least a minimal commitment to Corporate Social Responsibility and sustainable development. She remembered her grandfather saying, 'If you want to rebel against a system, you have to do it from within. You can't just stand up and shout that you disagree.' She knew the path would be arduous, and that she might have been changed by the system before she would be able to change it. Not too far down the road, reality asserted itself:

I've only been here for three years, and I have become slightly disenchanted. I have a much more realistic vision now of the organization's work and what trade-off can or can't be made. I think that is probably good, understanding how things work, because then you are more able to progress within a system, and get what you want out of it. If your views are too idealistic, you are unlikely to get to the bottom of something. But I think I have become a lot more cynical, maybe this is just growing up.

She was now willing to prepare for a period in her life when the excitement of career and increasing influence would replace her need to nurture her deeper intention.

The act of taking over a leadership function seems to create a new environment in which new structures and new patterns of relationship create a new framework for the shaping of identity. And in this chemistry the theme of the journey develops, most often beneath the surface. Experiences are not always easy to interpret – they do not follow the script we mean them to follow. We hit severe obstacles on our path and arrive at crisis points in our careers. Sometimes a person's path can change in a moment. There is no need to indulge in prolonged contemplation about the rights and wrongs of the choices you've made along your path. But it is worth looking for the common thread running through events, and trying to figure out the emotional connection to your deeper values. This helps you see that crises and times of disorientation are openings – they remind you of your heart and they push you into a new realm of life.

Gerard's career had always worked out. He grew up in France and when he was a young boy he loved adventure books. He loved adventures in nature most of all. Jacques Cousteau was his absolute favourite. There was something about being in tune with nature that had always fascinated him. When he was a teenager he read a poem by Kipling, in which an older man talked to a young man about how to be in the world. It impressed him that he would be a real man if he succeeded at being at ease with people, whether they were paupers or kings, then he would be a man. In Gerard's emotional world it was clear that everything was linked to everything else, that he was linked to the bigger world and that being at ease with the world was a form of harmony where no power prevailed. Being interested in science Gerard chose to complete a degree in engineering. He joined a multinational oil company, studied further, and his career progressed in a straightforward manner. He began to notice issues of power. Organizational culture required his participation in a dynamic and power-driven environment, and he did well. One manager with whom he felt really comfortable impressed him the most, because that manager always took other people into account, and valued fairness and a respect for different perspectives. He genuinely cared about other people's thoughts. However, Gerard did notice that this man's career options were limited: the value he placed on the idea of connecting differed substantially from the other managers' priorities. But despite Gerard's unease about this observation, he kept building his career path until many years later when he moved into a higher and very responsible position. He now had a superior with whom he just could not get on. And he disliked his colleagues in a way he just couldn't explain. He did his best, but finally concluded that it would be better to change jobs. He moved on, got another job in the same company, but the discomfort from his previous job stayed with him:

> The experience pushed me to start thinking why am I here, why am I working for this company, what am I looking for, all those questions, for which, at that time, I had no answers.

Initially he took this period as a very negative time in his career, an unjustified block he couldn't explain. But over time he realized the importance of the experience – it had triggered an inquiry into deeper questions in his life. A couple of years later, Gerard decided to leave the multinational company and take a year off to reconsider his path and his genuine contribution.

As the theme of the quest unfolds, it encounters major challenges along the way. Sometimes the quest lies hidden behind more immediate life events, personal choices and professional careers, and sometimes the challenges to the quest are disguised as crises, frustration, depression, fear, apathy, cloudiness or reticence. Sometimes we know that something needs to be done, yet we are reluctant to make the effort. Or we do not know what it is we could do or stop doing. The mind finds numerous arguments to keep things the way they are. The uncertainty of a quest, the unpredictability of a journey seldom aligns with the way we have laid out our life. So we don't make the effort – out of fear, out of resistance to change, or out of a feeling that we don't have the time or energy to make the extra effort.

No matter what leadership position we hold, we stop leading genuinely the moment we lose our connection to our quest – because this was the very reason we embarked on the journey: the intention to contribute, to discover, to understand. Leading, I believe, has at its deepest core the intention to serve. If we disconnect from our deeper intention, from the values we intuitively hold, we get off track. We will more likely respond superficially to the world – we thrive on, and are driven by, power, influence and material wealth. There is nothing 'wrong' with success in its numerous forms as a positive response to our being. But if we have disconnected from our deeper values, we can become entangled in the strings that attach us to the more superficial attractions in the world.

One very clear indication that we are disconnected from our inner core is when our passion dries up, when reason has silenced the heart's voice and dreams are things of the past. The presence or absence of passion is an excellent measure of your closeness to or distance from your underlying quest.

In retrospect, Gerard noticed that he had lost his passion long before he finally decided to leave the company and reshape his professional life. He carried out his tasks well. He contributed to his company's performance and there was a clear indication from the company that his chances of climbing the corporate ladder were good. In the first years of his working life, he had been very passionate about what he was doing – not so much as a reflection on what the company was doing, but for himself. He could see his path. He was very driven, able to propose solutions and to advance projects. This gradually turned into an inner commitment to the company's course, but at the same time, his own passion slowly but surely dissipated:

> I was committed to do the job that I was asked to do correctly and as well as I could, but I couldn't find why I was doing it, so I was spending the time to do it and the energy to do it but about the why I had no idea, I only realized this much later.

Leading is expressing your creative potential, your ability to bring forth the world with others. If your heart is no longer involved, if your passion has disappeared, it is time to ask uncomfortable questions. If you have abandoned your quest because of life's pressures and a daily schedule over which you have no control, you are in danger of abandoning your deepest potential to lead and contribute. The pianist and management consultant Michael Jones says: '… the question 'Must I lead?' is a perennial question that can never be settled once and for all time.' I believe this is a crucial remark – no matter what leadership position we hold or do not hold. We lead when we bring our unique potential into the world, when we neither shy away from contributing our gifts to the world nor avoid learning from the world's responses. But this kind of leading is a choice that needs to be renewed every now and then. We don't always feel like taking up the challenge of leading from within, harnessing the truth of our deepest values. This might, at times, feel naïve, and we have no idea how to enact such leadership in our world. There are times when we have tuned into a movement of co-creation made by circumstances we partly created ourselves. We might officially lead, but in doing so we act as carriers of a series of events over which we have little influence and that are pulling us along without us actually leading consciously. The need to service the identity we have built around ourselves in private and professional life prevents us from questioning the status quo, our contribution, and our way of leading. We tend to forget that leading is a creative act, no matter how structured the task appears to be, and that this creative energy needs renewal, regularly, consciously:

> Leading from our gifts is an art and, as with all [of the] art, is not only something we choose, but a calling that also chooses us. In making this choice, we become the ground upon which the forces of fear and contraction work against those of growth and expansion. In this fire our gifts gain the substance and the resilience to serve and also withstand the world. (Jones, 2000, p. 15)

Bringing the creative urge back into your life consciously is not always easy. Creativity has its own rhythms and dynamics. It requires phases of non-action – not something we have many opportunities to do in the daily rush of events. So, while searching for your earliest intention, you might also take the time to unearth what your pattern of creativity is. When we are creative, our heart is involved, we feel closer to life, and no matter how aware of it we are, we feel closer to our deepest values. People are different, so the ways that enable their creativity to flow are different.

Allowing your creative expression to well up from a deeper source requires emptiness within. This can mean a mind that rests in silence; it can take the form of withdrawal, into nature, into yourself, into a busy crowd you are somehow separated from. It is anything that allows an inward process of connection. Remember – when you connect with yourself, you connect with the world. And when you really connect with the world, you connect with yourself (we all know this energy when we fall in love). This inward-looking state is one of contraction. This is not necessarily a comfortable process – all artists know this. The void is also a place of vulnerability, insecurity and self-doubt. But it cannot be *avoided*. The chaos within is the breeding ground for a new creation. Expect trouble and don't expect easy answers. Welcome the very thing you would rather ignore: uncomfortable questions, rough times, unforeseen conflicts, and a lack of clarity. A new cycle of expansion usually rises from a time of chaos or emptiness. When we learn to integrate this more consciously into our lives, it will be less stressful and cause less unexpected discomfort. Then there is less of a need to enact outer crises, because we've integrated the need for contraction into our daily schedules. Internal shifts usually happen during periods of contraction. After a period of contraction, a new connection with the world forms. Sometimes the world looks different, we see things we have not seen before, and familiar things look different. We walk differently in the world. Our creative urge has been nourished, we become inventive, we make things happen, we plan new endeavours, and we bring forth the world. The result of contraction is always some kind of change – in our life, in our organization, something new manifests when we follow our creative urge and combine it with the creative urges of those around us.

CHAPTER ONE: UNFOLDMENT

Once the new creation, the idea, the structure, the physical change, the new relationships have taken root in the world, the phase of expansion slows down and finally rests, as it has come into being. It has created a new pattern in the world – different connections and different relationships. We often take this as the end point of creation. But it is not. It is just the mirror of our co-creative urge – the physical world reflects our creative impulses.

When we are able to complete the creative cycle consciously, we move into a different phase of contraction – this time deliberately and not alone. We consciously engage the system we helped to create into reflection, we actively invite feedback, and we foster collective contemplation. We create a space for resonance, deeper thoughts and truthful conversations. We ask, is our creation, and our co-creation, a meaningful response to what needs doing in the world, in this society, in this organization, in this family? This is a space rarely considered important in the professional world – it seems to be just a waste of time. But if it is missing, the cycle of creativity remains incomplete. We ourselves might end up creating and creating, inspired by success and driven by the attraction to power, influence, impact and self-image. The danger is that we'll run dry, lose our passion, disconnect from our heart, and above all, lose people because we are too preoccupied with our own creation, our own development.

We cannot know on our own what needs doing. Collective reflection is probably the most neglected aspect in leadership creativity. The importance of this second contraction phase of the creative process in fostering collective and individual learning in the sense of enfolding experience back into consciousness is often underestimated. It allows collectively generated insight to take its roots in the individual. It invigorates an internal expansion. It unfolds or expands in our individual consciousness, changes the structure of our thinking, reframes our identity and creates a new starting point for another creative wave to well up.

CHAPTER ONE: UNFOLDMENT

> *The creative process is continually occurring ... We are always somewhere on this wave in every part of our life ... We are surrounded and interpenetrated by a pulsating universal wave of creation. We are of it, we are it, it is us. It flows through us, and we flow through it. There is no end and no beginning. We create it as it creates us. There is no initiator. There is only the creative wave of life that is constantly unfolding and enfolding. (Brennon, 1988, p. 311)*

We know this by our tendency to avoid stagnation, contraction, the void. But if we begin to see the creative process as a whole, as a cycle requiring phases of different qualities, and not only as our inner drive being fulfilled by outward success, then we can put the pieces of our quest together in a different way. There are periods when we move in uncharted territory. They can be filled with excitement, yet accompanied by fears and self-doubt. There are moments when we lose direction. There are sometimes long phases when we trudge through life without being at all sure that we're doing the right thing. This is all part of the journey and cannot be avoided. But if you decide to revive your quest, you need to observe and accept it.

Edith worked for seven years in the social service structure in New York's Bronx, living her dream to promote equality: 'I found unbelievable passion. I was caring and doing unusual things and needed tremendous humility.' But there came a time when she hit obstacles in the most unexpected ways, and experienced a profound disappointment. Her passionate contribution ceased to align with people and reality. She was put in charge of a project, and while she had a strong connection to her clients in the Bronx, she encountered difficulties with colleagues in the social service structure, people she perceived as being more interested in money, status and position. She began to feel hugely disconnected, her spirit was lost, her passion dead. She got caught in a political intrigue, was outmanoeuvred by somebody else and finally left the service. She felt that something within her had been killed.

Not long after, she decided on a complete turnaround – she moved from psychology to technology and from the social services to business. This forced her to push the values she held deeply into the background and to apply the very rules she had been rebelling against for so long, but it also opened up an entirely new arena of her life.

Crises are also openings. We might not be willing to see this in the very moment they occur. But if you look back with a little bit of patience, you might find that your crises were forced contractions and, therefore, openings into new creative phases. You just couldn't avoid the downsides. Thus, reflection as a means to live the contraction phases of leadership creation more consciously, both individually and collectively, could be a cornerstone for reconnecting with your creative urge. Robert Greenleaf more intuitively recommends this as 'withdrawal' to re-orient oneself and calls it the art of 'systematic neglect' (Greenleaf, 1977, p. 19).

Again, people are different, and so are their leadership journeys. There is no one model, there is no recipe. Some people are at their most creative in solitude. Some need to be nourished by regular encounters with nature. Others only become enthused when they can connect with other people. They need to feel a deep human cord, a certain energy that is invoked by contact with other people.

When you look at your own leadership journey you might begin to find coherence, a meandering development with outer events triggering inner transformation and vice versa. Your identity, as a person and as a leader, has been, and is, under construction. If you look closely, you might be able to find a theme or a recurrent pattern that surfaces regularly and consistently. There is a story at the bottom of this theme. Before you try to overcome recurrent patterns that you have identified as negative, look more closely. They might contain clues to what your quest is about. You might be holding on to a deeper value that, if brought more into consciousness, would smooth your path and help you to be more at ease with the world.

Samson went to university after he had been released from prison. He studied in Ethiopia and in Europe. A new world opened up. The warrior in him was silenced by the experience of the military power in his country. He was careful to not repeat his way of fighting the system that had brought him into prison and that he would have now judged as naivety. Later in his life he joined the Faculty of Economics of the University of Addis Ababa, until he had a dispute that asked of him to either surrender to an organizational requirement that would have compromised his values or leave. Samson decided to resign:

> I realized that truth does not count. You will not win a case because you have truth with you. I did subject myself and my family to material problems. But it also showed me that without having been conscious about it then, I am driven by the quest for truth. The preparedness to stand behind the truth despite penalties and consequences is part of my leadership quest. That is what I see in myself. I also learned that you will not fail so long as you are internally balanced and solid. What matters is the coherence in yourself. That coherence gives you strength to surmount problems and gives you [the] capacity and ingenuity to be creative and find a new course in life.

There is a core of our identity that seems to remain unchanged throughout our leadership journey. Identity forms not so much as a result of an existing, unchangeable, persisting self, but as a result of a constitutional mental and physical structure emerging with a high degree of coherence in interaction with the world. It is obvious that reflection plays a crucial role in the transformative process of forming one's leadership identity, whatever form it takes. We often learn and reconnect with our deeper quest only at 'the edge of chaos'. We integrate humility and the reconciliation with our imperfect humanness in small doses into our identity. Our mental structures determine perception. We make sense of the world according to our experience. Our identity is the lens through which we look into the world. In its core, all this is formed during the early journey.

Patterns of thinking and subsequent action emerge from childhood and adolescence. The deeper initial intention forms. The quest begins. Patterns of action or thought are constituted and reconstituted in continuous reciprocal interaction between our individual mind and the structural context surrounding us – other people, the world. Patterns of thinking sometimes impede, sometimes facilitate learning. *The more we defend a certain rigid identity the less we learn.* It becomes more difficult to transcend experience, so we get stuck in it. It clouds our path and we expect more of the same. We re-enact similar patterns.

A Glimpse into Theory: Self and Identity

The construction (and possibly deconstruction) of one's own identity is a lifelong process. We generally assume that the deeper character of a person is difficult to change. This might be true to some extent: and what I argue here about the initial deeper intention also assumes that there is something we have created within that remains relatively stable in its core. But it is also important to realize that our identity is not fixed despite how much we are inclined to defend it. Our identity is constantly changing in response to experience. Our Self is a process and not a status quo (Macy, 1991a). For Joanna Macy, the identity of a person does not reside in an enduring substance or 'self', but in the actions of the person, and the choices he or she makes. They shape behaviour and experience, which, in a reciprocal loop, shape the person's identity (Macy 1991a, p. 173). In such a view, the self is not separate; it lives in its relationship to others as recipients of one's action. Long ago, Martin Buber described the same relational aspect of the 'self' in his essay on I and Thou when he said: 'In the beginning is relation' (Buber, 1970, p. 69). He reminds us that no identity, no self is thinkable without the innate longing for the 'You'. 'Man becomes I through a You. What confronts us comes and vanishes, relational events take shape and scatter, and through these changes crystallizes, more and more each time, the consciousness of the constant partner, the I-consciousness' (Buber, 1970, p. 80).

If one sees the organizing principle of the universe as relationship (Jaworsky, 1996), concepts of self and identity that neatly demarcate a person, and which assume the development and personal growth of a person to be mainly self-created and self-determined, become questionable. Identity, in a participatory universe, is not only highly co-created by relationships, it is actually part of these relationships, part of an infinite network of cause and effect. 'Identity is inseparable from relationship' (Helgesen, 1995 p. 16). Is, then, the assumption of a distinct leadership identity illusionary? Despite all attempts at personal mastery, can a leader only become what he or she is because of others?

If one sees identity in its relational aspect, one could describe it as a set of interconnected patterns, a network in communication with other networks. The development of these patterns in connectivity takes place continually, yet it only becomes observable and conscious with growing self-reference. When awareness and attention become more prominent, a person begins to communicate with herself about the pattern of identity and begins to understand the process of co-creation between her and the world differently.

A manager from a multinational company describes this as follows:

'I always assumed that identity is a relational and volatile thing. Identity is shaped by and inherently is an aspect of relationships, but it is so that you have a choice about the quality of the relationship. Identity for me is a pattern. There is always a choice to be made, how to relate and when to relate and then it deeply affects the evolution of the pattern. I guess in some ways there is a core that is not immutable, but more static than the rest of the pattern and that core can be shifted but requires a great deal of awareness before it begins to move. And that core is tied consciously or unconsciously to the world out there or to the perception of the world out there. I tried to determine how much self awareness is part of that ability to see the pattern. It would almost be like becoming aware of the constant flowing, being able to see the centre of the pattern, the initial primal pattern that one needs to be conscious of, in order to maybe shift and integrate in a different way.'

What this manager points out very profoundly is the role of reflection in enabling the flexibility of identity to such a degree that the person can learn in response to experiences. Attachment to a certain image of oneself makes it more difficult to adapt and to participate in the evolutionary process. Holding on to a particular image of our identity could possibly prevent us from seeing the whole and our part in it. But at the same time, there seems to be a deeper core in which the superficial life experiences need to be integrated, one by one.

Margaret Wheatley reminds us that the self is not a fixed feature, but that it is the means through which we experience, understand and interpret the world. 'We see the world through who we are. All living beings create themselves and they use that 'self' to filter new information and co-create their worlds. We refer to this self to determine what's important for us to notice. Through the self, we bring form and meaning to the infinite cacophony of data that always surrounds us' (Wheatley, 1999, p. 167).

In the dilemma between needing to become aware of oneself and falling prey to the illusion of maintaining a certain image of oneself, it might prove helpful to approach the issue of self and identity as a process of continuous change. If one sees the world in terms of relationship and not so much, as we are used to doing, in terms of substance, then personal identity becomes an emergent and constantly changing phenomenon influencing its environment and constantly being influenced by it.

Because of apparent reality and the structure of our sense organs, we do perceive separate objects, we create abstractions, including that of a separate self, and we start believing that these objects belong to an objective and independent reality. Capra concludes: '… we need to think systemically, shifting our conceptual focus from objects to relationships. Only then can we realize that identity, individuality, and autonomy do not imply separateness and independence.' (Capra, 1996, p. 295).

Identity, then, can only be approached as a mental pattern in constant interaction as part of a web of relationships, reciprocally co-created and supported by a physical structure, the body. This mental pattern never just exists; it constantly creates itself and is created, ever changing and fluid. It is, perhaps, the essence or the quality of this seemingly maintained and, on the surface level, slowly changing pattern, that, as Norbert Wiener puts it 'is the touchstone of our identity... We are but whirlpools in a river of ever-flowing water. We are not stuff that abides, but patterns that perpetuate themselves' (Wiener, 1967, p. 130).

There is a balance to find – the more we construct ourselves as open to feedback, the more we will be able to transcend experience and come closer to forgiveness and compassion for our own and others' imperfect humanness. And there is a core to sustain – the deeper values we hold, values of the heart, need to be brought back to life and nourished. They are our connection to the collective human consciousness, to the human heart. On the surface of the quest are outer events, career paths, achievements. Underlying these is a deeper journey. It is vital to access this deeper quest because when it is dormant, we run at half our natural speed and contribute a fraction of what we are and what we could be. In a way, though we may be very active in the outside world, we shy away from our real leadership capacity. We might be good at something, and we perform, but do we lead?

No matter what causes reflection, outside events, inner or outer crises, a question, an encounter with somebody else or a slow process of dissatisfaction with one's life, at some point on the leadership journey a moment of stillness seems to occur that sets a different tune. Questions become louder and there is a demand for inner space, time, and the freedom to think into a different direction.

CHAPTER ONE: UNFOLDMENT

Inquiry, the art of asking questions in order to find truth, understanding and meaning, is certainly as old as humankind. One of the documented rhetorical questions of the Buddha in ancient India was: What is the purpose of inquiry? '[It] … is to seek for the absolute unity which underlies all seeming diversity.' (Oliver, 1971, p. 76). Now this response might be too far from our daily reality. But, at its core, it has a meaning that is important to contemplate: in ancient India the purpose of inquiry was not to find a solution to a current problem. A question or set of questions was the vehicle for opening the mind to a deeper understanding of the world. An inquiry does not necessarily follow rational logic, it can rest on intuition: 'The individual cannot think his way to understanding; he must feel his way toward it. The end sought is not objective clarification, but subjective insight' (ibid., p. 76).

Inquiry, if understood in such a way, can be an aid on the road to the perception of coherence. A process of inquiry increases our ability to step into the unknown. This is not a culture we nurture in our professional lives. Very few corporate or institutional environments invite good questions instead of good answers. Good questions do not have immediate answers. Coaches know this phenomenon: if you have asked a question that cannot be answered right away you have opened the person to change. Unanswered questions are faithful – they accompany the person until they have been answered, much later, not always directly and not always consciously. The mind is constructed to keep unanswered questions in the forefront of consciousness, particularly those that have touched the heart. Finding the questions that cannot be answered immediately is a vital component of our developmental path. This can be unsettling rather than comforting: the least that is expected of a leader of today's organization is that he or she does not know the answer or searches for questions that, for him or herself or for others, cannot be answered straight away.

Inquiry underscores uncertainty and an acceptance of uncertainty. Engaging in inquiry means to be willing to look into what one does not know or understand, and to search for the understanding of what others see that might differ from one's own point of view. It invites dialogue, with oneself and with others. Real and deeper inquiry, into ourselves, into life or into a situation, requires the ability to listen. Only when a person suspends the urge to find a quick explanation for what is, when silence is allowed to take space, only then can inquiry lead to the depths of life's data. What is known and interpreted as meaning this or that can be dismantled and re-synthesized. In a difficult-to-answer question is a request to open beyond the old interpretations and take a fresh look at what one thinks one already knows. An attentive inquiry is likely to transform our habitual tendency to listen only to what we already know and overcome our inertia to go beyond conforming our memory's choices to the meaning we made up long ago. The ability to inquire is to perturb and penetrate this ordinariness of human explanation, to go beyond it into the unknown and open and allow, with the question, a possibility to emerge that would not do so otherwise. It is a commitment to new possibilities of life.

In that the question is an opening to a new form of life, it actually allows the re-organization of our thought patterns – a prerequisite for something new to develop. Inquiry is not a technique, it is a way of being. It requires courage, the permission for empty spaces in our leadership journey and above all the willingness to learn and to listen to oneself and others. Or as Robert Greenleaf puts it: '… only a true natural servant leader automatically responds to any problem by listening first. When one is a leader, this disposition causes one to be seen as servant first. This suggests that a non-servant who wants to be a servant might become a natural servant through a long arduous discipline of learning to listen.' (Greenleaf, 1977, p. 17). Questions that allow the discovery of the world within and without, asked from an inner attitude of respect, genuine interest and openness to discovery, are gateways to understanding the coherence of life and the deeper quest of our leadership journey. They can be the beginning of a healing process.

Paul is a manager in a multinational company. He has spent 27 years there, with great enjoyment and sometimes greater ambivalence. He has held various leadership positions, but only in the last couple of years has he developed a different attitude to space and reflection:

> Questions have actually caused deep reflection … I often go for a walk and think about them and come back, and a week later I read them again. What I found great in questions is that I noticed … there has been a consistency in my leadership journey. Deep down inside I have not changed what I feel I want to be, and what my journey is about. So my thinking, my depth of feeling, my intent, I don't believe it has altered in 30 years. The way I have approached turning that feeling, or thinking or intent into practical action, has definitely wavered throughout the years, but has become stronger and more consistent from the heart pull or action, than in the early days where it was a mixture of the heart and the head. My quest was to help people develop as people, and access the capabilities they never knew they had. I didn't know this when I started out on my journey, I couldn't have articulated it but that is how it felt.

The developmental path of a leader is shaped by the way questions are posed and transformed as they inform the inner and outer search. The way of re-organizing memory through inquiry influences the art of finding new possibilities in life. There is an assumption here – the ability to listen, to create empty spaces, the courage to venture into the unknown and the establishment of a continuous inner dialogue have as much influence on our developmental paths as external events.

Inquiry helps us transcend experience. The more we are not just driven in our leadership journey, but able to observe what is happening while it is happening, or at least, to reflect in retrospect, the more our choices will be made contextually – that is, with increasing perception of the whole. When we gradually become alert to the deeper dimension of our path we will also perceive other people's paths in a more differentiated way. We might notice principles operating in the lives of others that are similar to our own. We might notice that the theme of our journey survives. It is the underlying quest that is unique to us, because we hold it in this world and it is eternal, because it expresses one particular form of a collective human consciousness.

This is how Samson expresses it in his early fifties:

> I believed all along when the moment of reckoning comes my inner self and energy [are] driven by the search for truth and equality of human beings young and old, short and tall, fat and thin, poor and rich. I have never submitted to the pressures of power, be it political or economic. Sometimes I feel that I am foolish. Because I think that truth matters and works but when I 'wake up' and look around it is not truth that is leading the world, but rather pragmatism – playing the dance of powers. Despite this occasional 'waking up' however I have remained a rebel to [what] I think does not represent the truth and to anything that questions the equality of human beings. If I were to have my way, my choice would be to join with similar minds and hearts around the world and work towards creating a world where *truth* holds and matters and where human beings get at least a minimum security of

existence and are treated equally irrespective of status. Where everybody enjoys the same degree of confidence in being and living in the common home – the world, where the world of inequality is replaced by the world of equality and people have more opportunity to live a life of their choosing.

CHAPTER ONE: UNFOLDMENT

Reflections

Can you remember a daydream or thoughts you had when you were young (childhood, adolescence or when you were a young adult) that had anything to do with wanting to change the world, wanting to do something for the world (be it small or big), helping people or nature, or being somebody special with particular influence on the world? How did this dream or thought come about? What was it connected to? Which events preceded it or surrounded it? What was it? Did it get lost? Were there different dreams?

Was there any person or figure from a book or a movie with whom you identified? Why? What qualities did this person or figure have?

When you were a teenager, was there anything that fascinated you a great deal, or something you were searching for, a quest you felt you needed to be on, or something you wanted know or be or become?

CHAPTER ONE: UNFOLDMENT

Chapter 1: Summary

- Reconnecting with our deeper initial intention is not only paramount for our leadership journey, but a good guide in finding our deepest values.
- If we look for hunches and clues, we can examine our young leadership story, our dreams, admirations, encounters, thoughts, secrets, turning points, and insights.
- We can relax – this is not about acquiring more skills. Discovering our own unfoldment is more like peeling off layers of memory to unearth our true nature, just us, the way we are. This can help us to redefine our contribution as a leader and to open to a more meaningful life.
- No matter where we are on our journey, there is always the recurrent question: must I lead? Rather than being led by structures and circumstances, the core of our leading calls us to lead from our heart and our deeper intention.
- It is worth to ourselves and to the world that we consciously integrate our deeper values into our leadership journey. The world desperately needs us to unpack and live them. Everybody counts.

CHAPTER TWO

PARTICIPATION

Mandy grew up in a small town in Michigan in the United States. When she was six years old she invented a game she was very fond of playing. She was in charge of the game in the playground. It was called 'Mrs Idiotic', but she didn't know the meaning of the word. She picked it because it was so unusual and nobody knew it. The game went like this: Mandy would sit at the top of the jungle-gym where she could see all the kids from a vantage point. All of them were part of her community, they were *her* people and she would tell them what to do. They would go out and catch other kids for Mandy's group and then put them in her castle, symbolized by a tree. If the captives were really rebellious and if they broke the rules, her people would usher them to a different part of the playground. Mandy loved this game, she played it for more than a year and the others would readily join in. Nobody ever came up with a different game. Her supremacy was never challenged. She was in charge and she loved it – she felt lightness around her role in this. The shock came when she finally asked an adult what the word 'idiotic' meant. Learning the meaning of the word was such a shock and embarrassment that she never played the game again.

Today Mandy is in her early fifties. She owns a successful consulting company that focuses on organizational change and leadership coaching. She comments:

> When I look back on this childhood experience, I realize that it triggered a long phase of denying leadership, not putting myself in a situation where I could make the choices and I was in charge. The memory was too embarrassing: the word idiotic, but also the kind of command and control style, very

autocratic, where I would tell other kids what to do. This was not the way I wanted to be.

A moment of insight can change a life and a leadership journey. It cannot be denied – leading is a certain way of 'being in relationship' that differs from 'not-leading'. It brings the person more directly and more responsibly into the participation in and generation of life. A positive response to the impact of one's voice and action is both frightening and lightening. It can become addictive.

Mandy's feeling of discomfort about her leadership role as Mrs Idiotic was a lasting experience. In retrospect, she noticed that there was a reflection of this experience in her consultancy practice. At the core of her work now was inclusion. She was known for her way of convincing even the most command-and-control style of leaders of the need for participation and inclusiveness. But she also noticed a pattern in her business life:

> People who ask me to be in support of them are often people whom I see as those who are most unforgiving or deeply wounded or frightened within themselves. Somebody jokingly said to me, 'Whenever you talk about your clients, they are all absolute bastards'. And I said, 'Some of them are, not all of them, but a lot of them'. And part of what I know is that I am drawn to extremes, the disenfranchised and those without a voice in a larger world, those who are small and disenfranchised and feel unheard and, on the other end of the spectrum, the very people who are most responsible for perpetrating the kinds of systems that put people there.

The issue of participation and inclusion has been on the agenda of organizational learning and change for many years. It seems that participation is a powerful emerging alternative in the governing structures of businesses in some parts of the world, and although its uptake in businesses might still be slow and subject to the pressure of performance and business survival, the general direction seems to be towards organizational governance structures and stakeholder engagement that allow increased levels of participation. This is a response to changing organizational structures, changing models of leadership and the demands for more sustainable business practices.

Participatory leadership acknowledges that the totality of people in an organization is a flux of differing perspectives and emotionally charged agreements and disagreements, and most probably also a continual balancing of values and interests. There is no single truth or final answer. Quite different from Mrs Idiotic's approach, leading from a new paradigm of participation conveys an art of designing communication processes which allow differences to emerge and build consensus at the same time. Leadership is no longer tightly bound to a certain position; it is no longer a title bestowed on a few. It is a role anyone can engage in while pursuing a larger agreed-upon goal. But there is something special about the person who has been entrusted with a positional leadership role. To ignore this would be naïve. The way a person entrusted with leadership holds his or her role, makes a difference. The way she holds herself and others is crucial, too. There is no way out – because of their actual or perceived position, leaders bring forth reality differently from non-leaders.

I do not know where you are heading as a leader. But I believe that there is a responsibility that goes far beyond the task. It even goes far beyond being responsible for people. It is a responsibility for the emergence of reality. Not that you are creating reality on your own; you always do this co-creatively. But there are different patterns for co-creation. Mrs Idiotic's approach is one. Another is to create a pattern of communication that supports people expressing their innermost voice and creating a space where people feel they participate as leaders themselves in the unfolding of something meaningful. Between the two approaches are many varieties of leadership. Which end of the spectrum contributes more to sustainability? Mrs Idiotic's approach can be highly efficient, it can save lives, but can it create life? Can it sustain life in the long run? The point is crucial when you begin to think about your contribution to sustainability.

A form of leadership communication that fosters the feeling of inclusiveness creates a space in which people stay personally engaged. You fuel the life energy in people. It also enables people to create a larger capacity for contradictions and differences in opinion – a capacity very much needed for the kind of leadership that is required to move towards more sustainability in the world. When people feel included, they experience respect. This makes it easier to respect others, too, and to acknowledge non-compliant views, difference and diversity. All of this is an important prerequisite for sustainability in a globalized world.

A Glimpse into Theory: Participation in the Evolutionary Process

The leadership journey is a learning cycle with constant fluctuation between stability and instability, the re-organization of identity on ever higher and more complex levels and the integration of experience. This does not take place in isolation, but as (more or less conscious) participation in the process of a collective 'bringing forth of the world'. In that way, every individual pathway is a fractal of the evolutionary process. The theory of living systems suggests that life has an inherent tendency to create novelty (Capra, 1996, p. 226). Evolution is not perfect, it is more an imperfect creative learning process, of which we are part and which we influence. It is a never-ending process of making order from chaos. Things go wrong, developments become dangerous to the sustenance of life, and this creates pressure to re-organize and rebalance. And in this way, imperfection leads to progress (Sahtouris & Lovelock, 2000, p. 296). Nature tries out what the best next steps could be and develops accordingly.

Living systems are always parts of larger wholes. Although one can distinguish the parts in any living system, the nature of the whole is different from the mere sum of its parts. Every organism, animal, plant, micro-organism, or human being is an integrated whole, a living system. Parts of these organisms are, of course, living systems in themselves. Throughout the living world, we find systems nesting within other systems. And living systems also include communities of organisms. These may be social systems like a family, a school, an organization, a village, a city or larger ecosystems (Capra, 1996, p. 213). Life, in such a view, is a certain way of constantly arranging and rearranging matter and energy within and between this vast array of living systems, and it seems that life on Planet Earth is the most complex evolution of this interaction of matter and energy.

An important feature of living systems is their relationship patterns ordered in the form of a network with constant internal communication. Although systems can be organizationally closed (for example, we as human beings) and have visible boundaries (for example, our skin), viewed from a larger context it is almost arbitrary where to draw the boundaries of a system: each boundary functions as a different level of the whole or larger system. There is a degree of autonomy and self-rule, but looked at from a distance, every whole is interdependently embedded in larger wholes. There is a need for every whole to balance its own autonomy with the rules of the larger whole (Sahtouris & Lovelock, 2000, p. 51). From a living system's point of view, the essential feature in the Universe is relatedness (Capra, 1996, p. 173) and some argue that this is much more fundamental than 'thingness' (Jaworsky, 1996, p. 57).

Life has a fundamentally holarchic nature, with a continual dialogue going on among the relatively autonomous wholes. This kind of conversation seems to be critical to the survival of the larger whole as well as of its parts. No living system can be independent. The dialogue or negotiation takes place between the needs and identity of the smaller whole and the needs and the identity of the larger whole. Relative autonomy is constantly negotiated within the larger whole. We as human beings are part of this ongoing negotiation process. Elisabeth Sahtouris suggests that '... we can only understand ourselves as humans by trying to understand our co-evolution with the rest of nature' (Sahtouris & Lovelock, 2000, p. 264).

The larger whole functions like an enormous network in constant interaction. This network is non-linear, connected in any possible direction and built in such a way that constant feedback is guaranteed. The crucial point when considering sustainability is that living systems theory suggests a distinct difference between nature's networks and organizations, communities and societies created by humans. The network of nature is composed in such a way that it regulates and organizes itself. There is no hierarchy, but a constant co-creation taking place (Capra, 1996, p. 218). Nobody is leading this, nothing steers the process. The structures of larger wholes arise from the interactions and interdependence of smaller wholes and vice versa. From within such a paradigm, larger systems, for example organizations or societies, cannot be seen as a collection of individuals who have come to live and function together. They can better be described as a whole interacting with itself, while this whole interacts with other wholes, and all of them with a larger whole, and so on.

In the view of living systems theory, the fatal illusion of independence has lead to a distorted view of reality with an enormous impact on the history of humankind. The lack of awareness about the planet functioning as a whole (including humanity) has created the notion of scarcity and the need for competition 'The social view of individual people pitted against one another in ... struggles makes little more sense as an ideal than the notion that our bodies' cells are competing with one another to survive in hostile bodies. It is simply no longer useful or productive to see ourselves as forced to compete with one another to survive in a hostile society surrounded by hostile nature' (Sahtouris & Lovelock, 2000, p. 109). From such a perspective, the world in its diversity is brought into existence by all the living systems involved. There is no hidden force. Participation and interdependence are the organizing principles. Everything belongs together, humankind, the world. No actor can escape this essential togetherness. Elisabeth Sahtouris suggests the term 'mutual consistency' as a description for the 'worked-out balance' or harmony through dialogue and negotiation (Sahtouris & Lovelock, 2000, p. 23) within smaller and larger wholes. The key to such a negotiated balance is diversity, which in nature is a crucial requirement for the relative stability (or sustainability) of a system (ibid., p. 12 and p. 297). The greater the diversity, the more sustainable a system becomes in the long run. This means that the system has a higher capacity for renewal.

CHAPTER TWO: PARTICIPATION

Leading has many faces. The history of humankind is witness to this. It is easy to determine what kind of leadership was not sustainable in the long run – though it might have been effective in the short term. It is much more difficult to identify the examples for leadership that centred on sustainability. There are too many factors in the equation. But this does not mean we stop thinking about it. Leading for sustainability is not something we really know how to do yet. Not every admired leader has created sustainability. Not every person doing good in the world has been a good leader. There are no easy answers to questions like these, just an invitation to inquire into the world and into your own future possibilities.

I believe it is important to review our leadership in its contribution to mutual consistency. How can we bring forth reality in a more life-sustaining way, in the short-term, the long-term, over the span of our life, during every single day? What is the larger whole that I am willing to contribute to in a sustaining way? How large, how small is it? How do I lead? In what way do I or do I not contribute to the sustainability of the larger whole (there may be many)? What is my way of creating sustainability (renewal, learning, diversity)? What is the next-level 'whole' that I really want to sustain? How much am I concerned with humanity as a whole and with the community close to me? How do I participate in this unfolding of evolution?

If you find these questions too far away from your daily reality, and impossible to answer, you could consider an easier question.

What would a leader be like and how would s/he act for you to be willing to follow (not in war, not in emergency)?

Place yourself in the position of a voluntary follower. You might come up with the idea that, if you had a choice, you would not want to follow anybody. This is fine. It might be worthwhile inquiring into that. Or, you might have a feeling of how it could be to be led and to grow at the same time. Or you might remember persons

CHAPTER TWO: PARTICIPATION

who led you (or taught you) whom you admired. Whatever comes to mind around this question can lead you deeper into the theme of sustainability.

One would imagine that the answer to this question is culturally bound. Yet when I talked to leaders from different cultures, different religious backgrounds, different geographical areas, and different types of organizations, I found an amazing similarity in the essence of their responses. We all seem to know the core of leadership that is life-creating because we know how it feels when we are led by somebody who inspires our life force.

Lucia, who had joined a multinational energy company thought she would most probably follow somebody who would be best placed to lead for the collective good. For her, the person needed to be internally balanced, somebody with humour and a good heart:

> It must be somebody capable in his area with a mind that goes beyond the ordinary thinking. He or she should be inspirational in the sense of fostering my own capability to live my potential. I would be following somebody who is prepared to stand out from the crowd with courage, somebody who does what seems right not what is expected, but also somebody who would make space for me, who would listen attentively and make room for other people's feelings and thoughts. Somebody who would give me space and respect me.

Mandy, the American executive director of a consulting firm in the UK, found this:

> I think that I would welcome someone who would not hold leadership totally, someone who could share leadership with others and someone who would have [the] kind of humility that comes not from being self-restraining but from being

CHAPTER TWO: PARTICIPATION

pragmatically aware of humanity. The humility would come from [a] kind of grounded experience in living rather than a sense of greatness and vision; it would come from seeing life. I am drawn to leaders who have been through it ... not those who have been graced and gifted, more those who have seen life as hard and difficult and all aspects and have come through that and still have a great capacity to love and have a capacity to hope. The leader I could follow would not hold a vision so tightly that others can't share it, or a purpose so firmly that it cannot be embraced and then shaped by others.

Gerard, the French engineer and manager from a multinational company, saw it like this:

> The image I have of a leader I was prepared to follow is somebody with the function of a menhir ... you know these standing stones ... a menhir is something that is here to connect with the bigger stuff, whatever it is, with me, with the people around here. In a leader it is somebody who understands and can make people understand some of the connections between the greater universe or the whole and the individuals. So it is a capacity to connect. And a leader I was prepared to follow might actually be somebody who is able to make these connections with me, the individual, the follower and something I am looking for, my actual or my current understanding and feelings.

Anna, the head of a human resource department in a Swedish union, emphasized the role of freedom:

> For me a leader has to build up an atmosphere of freedom for everyone in the team, or the group, to grow within themselves

in their own space. When I look back I can see that when I have left an organization or I had conflict with leaders I was supposed to follow, it comes back to the fact that I hadn't felt free, that I was kept in place, restrained. So then I made an active choice to leave or I engaged in conflict, and sometimes the conflict was resolved and we would arrive at different terms, a different way to cooperate. So freedom is essential for me – as well as participation and acceptance. I also follow leaders who are committed and really engage in what they do, because this has the force to drive me.

The descriptions of who people are willing to follow form a tapestry of images depicting the kinds of leadership that create the feeling of aliveness within people. It seems to be the energy around values, truth and authenticity that would make people willing to follow. The examples might express dreams of a world of compassionate human interaction, but they are not naïve: these are people who have forged their careers and hold responsible positions. They highlight the core of the leadership endeavour: to be entrusted to lead, be it ideas or people, requires above and beyond all additional leadership skills, *the ability to contribute to life and other people's growth*. Hence, leading implies more than participation. It is a certain way of taking part in the unfolding of reality. We have choices. We are exerting our creativity in the world. We do influence. There is direction and from this comes responsibility. Whether we are committed to fulfill a task or to follow a vision, we want to change at least this small, defined part of the world.

If we begin to attend to the whole more consciously, we learn that this whole needs expression: but we cannot think on behalf of it. We need to ask. Processes of communication can either prevent such expression or they can foster it. Whether the diversity of the world is brought out in different views or not, the whole, in the sense of an underlying coherence, will press for emergence. When our form of communication prevents other people from expressing themselves rather than enabling them to do so, the very chaos we might have wanted to avoid starts surfacing on another level, in informal communication, in ineffective behaviour, disengagement or absence of commitment, loss of passion, disconnection. Then mutual respect usually declines.

Communication, as one of the ways a leader attends to the whole, requires admitting that we all construct our world through self-designed lenses. By doing so, we participate in creating the very world we seem to observe only as a given. Conscious communication processes that foster true inclusion (not false participation) enable this process of co-creation to become transparent, and in this very process, mutual understanding and respect increase. If we ensure that all voices are heard, we foster an atmosphere of respect and inclusion. By listening and observing first, you might be able to foster communication rather than block it. The purpose is to foster connection, and with that to bring forth the whole rather than simply to connect the parts. Communication is a space in which consciousness can change. If you begin to gradually attend to a wider whole, your participation in the unfolding of reality changes. Your awareness about the role of dialogic communication grows. You engage differently. There is a reciprocal effect. When you begin to listen more attentively, the way you voice yourself will change.

Form a very young age, Mandy was continuously involved in singing activities, both alone and in choirs, so that she grew up with the experience of her voice being strongly expressed and heard. For her, the ability to sing in a group was the experience of collective expression and attentiveness to the sound together:

> ...when we are attentive to each other and yet are still expressing ourselves individually. I think that that probably surpasses

all other experiences I have had in life about being part of a whole, and being able to express something deeper than myself, and knowing I was part of something larger.

When Mandy moved from the United States to Europe and took up a position in a bank, she stopped singing within six months. Her job could not accommodate it, she could not accommodate it. There was something about inner space – it was missing, so she could not sing. As she moved on in her professional career in the corporate world, she became very skillful in leading without being in a prominent leadership position, almost as if she had chosen a way of leading that would not require her to voice herself directly. While her capacity to sing was lying idle, she began to be attracted to the kind of power that did not put her on the spot, but moved other leaders in front with whose values and ways of being she could identify. She helped other leaders to succeed, she lent them her voice.

When you begin to communicate more consciously in the world, it can be helpful to reconstruct the history of your own voice first. All communication starts within yourself. It is all connected. If you have intentionally or unintentionally buried your early dreams and silenced the voice of your heart, the way you communicate with people can only touch the surface. You can neither reach out to your own wholeness nor bring forth wholeness around you. You cannot access the humanity of another person when you have not accessed your own humanity. Your deeper values, symbolically held in your early intention, your dreams, and your aspirations are gateways to your vitality in this world, your ability to create and to lead. Tracing the history of your voice is important. It takes you back to places you might want to leave untouched and forgotten for the rest of your life: the pain of a memory of wanting to be heard and feeling silenced; the embarrassing feeling of saying something of importance to you to a group of people who simply ignored you and continued with their conversation; the memory of a teacher scolding you and you feeling unable to defend yourself; the nightmare when you wanted to scream and you could not; the paper you submitted that you were proud of only to get a bad mark; the project proposal you designed and presented to the board and you never heard a response ;the occasion when you heard yourself speaking and had the feeling that this can't be me; the situation when you thought you really had a great idea, and it only harvested polite laughter. There is, presumably for each of us, a history of unspoken truth, ignored concern, sidelined contribution.

We learn from experience – withhold our honest opinion, avoid speaking from the heart, doubt our creative ability, and adjust the way we speak our voice to the conditions of the context we operate in. We can become tremendously successful at this. We might arrive at a point when we ask ourselves how long we will be able to afford not expressing our true voice. Finding your voice precedes the redefinition of your leadership contribution. It is a process requiring patience and persistence.

When Mandy consciously examined her successful consulting projects, she identified an interesting pattern. The most successful was a transformation process in a bank in one of the neighbouring countries. She had the background role of a consultant, yet her intention to ensure that the diversity of voices and concerns would be heard in the change process, was not only the core of the process design, but finally adopted as a guiding principle by the management in charge. The process was hugely successful, but she had to deal with a real crisis when the leadership team she was working with began to challenge her. They challenged her to actually stand in the limelight and not deny her upfront leadership skills. The moment of being forced to accept her upfront leadership role was a decisive moment of realizing a pattern that was keeping her from expressing her real voice:

> I think I did not want to show up as a leader, but they did not collude with me. They did not let my leadership remain inexplicable or in shadow. I absolutely had a voice of leadership in the business I was consulting, but I came from this angle of endless consultation and participation, and respect for differences in the organization, hearing the voices of all the people in the organization. I remember having a crisis, saying to the leadership team, I am not a leader, you are the leaders, you are the leadership team, I am just a vehicle. It took that team to take me on and say, this is bullshit, you are a leader, you are and have been and if not, you do not understand your actions in this context and the impact they are having in relationship to all of it and everyone. It is not a question of right or wrong, it simply is. And I have always acknowledged that that was the best work I have ever done.

It is not a once-off occasion when you suddenly begin to speak your true voice. It is a process of unfolding the courage to be really you. This takes time. If you trace the history of your voice, you might find moments when you attempted to speak from the heart, but it had no impact in the world. Or you might find other times when you were heard, but the voice you spoke did not really come from the heart. What we express as leaders, ideally, has its ground in our being, in the way we have established a relationship with ourselves and our innermost aspirations, beliefs or dreams. But the way we voice ourselves in the stream of daily reality that we participate in does not always come straight from the heart. I am not suggesting that you go against your common sense and risk your life's achievements by always voicing what you really think. But I do suggest that finding your voice is a search worthwhile undertaking. There will be no perfection, and the search might never really be completed, but it can result in gradually coming closer to your natural way of being in this world. It is, to coin a phrase, a process of de-fragmentation.

I grew up in a family with an older sister and a younger brother. My strangest childhood experience is that I felt I did not have a voice in this family – I was too different; somehow, inexplicably, I did not belong. I don't know if this began when I refused to speak in the language of adults until I turned four. It was not that I did not speak, I just spoke my own language and I needed my sister to translate to my parents. Much later, of course, I communicated normally, but the feeling of not being understood persisted. I was often teased by my father for not getting what was going on straight away. But there were no disabilities; I did extremely well at school.

Much later, when I was coordinating change management in a company, my core competency was in creating workshop settings and communicative spaces in which people could speak up, exchange ideas and create future designs. I also noticed that I had a real voice in the management team. What I said was often referred to and taken up by those in charge. This was flattering, but it was accompanied by a strange form of dissatisfaction. I got heard, more than I expected, but I felt fragmented, too. What I would have really found important to say, I could not say. There was a huge volume of knowledge and intuition inside me that I could not convey. I could not find the words I trusted to be understood. I simply sensed that people would not have taken me seriously.

Speaking our voice does not necessarily mean we become good communicators in the sense of an acquired set of communication skills. Such skills are important when we lead, but what I am referring to is the moment when we stop shying away from truly speaking from the heart. A leader's voice, spoken from the heart, can create

CHAPTER TWO: PARTICIPATION

a new order in a conversation and can open up new possibilities. In speaking, we create.

Our ability to enhance communication, viewed through this lens, has its roots in our relationship with our own voice, and our capacity to express that inner voice sufficiently. The more this inner process is in balance, the more likely we are to create the space for other people to express their innermost state, their values and beliefs. Communication, then, becomes a process of discovery of inner and outer reality, rather than an exchange of information. As entrusted leaders, rather than defining reality through our speaking, we would aim at creating a space in which reality can be collectively shaped through communication. Designing a space for communication to happen enables life's basic principle to flow: cycles of continuous feedback.

Philele holds a considerably high political and managerial position in the government of South Africa. He has a strong political background and is in his early fifties. His quest is and has always been the search for truth and justice. The passion of his quest has a long history:

> Some of the things I am passionate about can be a result of what I perceived in my family as unfair treatment of myself, by my old man, who punished a lot. It drove me to be very passionate about things like justice, and I think this is what ultimately drove me to do the things I am doing now; they are a result of this passionate sense of justice and fairness. For me, it shaped my life permanently. Even before later political sophistication I had a readiness to intervene, particularly in interpersonal relationships, and later this grew into bigger things.

Philele had a strong voice in intervention and leading. But it did not always render the results he intended. This, among others, triggered an inquiry into his own leadership:

All along I have been looking to leading, how people are leading and for a long time it did not occur to me, it hit me between the eyes, so to speak, that the issue is really about me. Now I am beginning to reflect and think more about how I myself am contributing to whatever is the situation around me. I look at myself more closely than was the case before. There is a form of anxiety – I found at times that I tend to stew in my own story and sometimes it creates a problem of communication, of understanding. So I have often not been as effective as I could have been if I had communicated differently. My leadership challenge is that I have to match the promptness of my communication with the timeliness of what needs to be said, instead of over-concentrating on the wisdom of saying so.

The history of voicing is different for each of us. While some of us do need to take the road of gradually speaking up and saying what we really mean deep from the heart, others might need to take the opposite road and gradually begin to understand the impact of their voice. How much life do we hinder because we do not speak our true voice? How much life do we hinder because we voice ourselves too forcefully, preventing others from daring to speak their voice? There is no recipe for balance, no guiding note prescribing how much we should or should not say. Both extremes, the shying away from our voice and the dominating others with our voice, rest on fear. The fear dissipates as we become more and more at home in the Universe. We become more at home with ourselves when we accept what is exactly as it is.

There is a connecting thread – from our early intention, our subconscious and conscious quest, the deeper values, the way we express our creativity through participation, and our connection to our voice from the heart. If you think about redefining your contribution as a leader, I believe it is worthwhile to track some of your experience of voicing yourself and to integrate the scattered pieces.

When you find the story of your voice, you know how it felt when you spoke from the heart. Not all life circumstances allow you to speak from the heart constantly. But if you embark on the journey of gradually creating more and more opportunities where you can speak from the heart, your leadership will change. You will become more vulnerable at times, and you will become more human. Finding, probably losing and re-finding your voice, is a process requiring the willingness to observe and to listen to yourself with greater attention. Again, this will have a reciprocal effect – you will notice how you begin to listen to others in a different way. Voicing and listening are essentially two ways in which we participate in the unfolding of reality. To become more attentive to how we are doing this will change the way we do it. We might begin to experience that voicing and listening cannot be separated. They are two aspects of the same movement. If we are willing to track our intentions, the history of our voice and the core of our quest, at some point we cannot but begin to voice ourselves in a different way. But we will also notice that we begin to hear different things as we gradually change the way we listen.

Paul moved from different management positions in a multinational company to the human resources department. He enjoyed the varied kind of work very much, as it gave him the freedom to express much more clearly the values he held, which he began to express more openly to those he serviced as an HR manager. Three times in the past decade, Paul had faced the dilemma of deciding between work and family priorities. And each time he chose the family:

> It was personally very difficult to manage. Having taken a stand three times, it actually feels good when you take a stand, but

the implications of that, in a kind of conventional way, I could say it spoiled my career. But I have come to modify that by saying I have learnt that where earlier I tended to see only the negative implications of it, I can now see the positive. I have become less judgmental towards myself and this extends to others. The learning had implications on my way of making decisions. Where previously I was very much a black-or-white person being sure that this or that would happen or would not happen, I now make decisions in a different way. I have learned from each stand I have taken. I feel much stronger, and from the strength comes confidence and the ability, if you like, to lead, both in my professional and in my private life. For me, leadership is no longer about imposing my thinking, it is about sharing my thinking and my views. I have begun to notice that I can open up to others what has been opened up to me. If I now help people to develop as people, I support them to lead rather than being led by circumstances, demands, and expectations. It is a major shift from what I think I should be doing, based on what others told me to do, to what I really want to do.

For Paul, this meant being able to be more truly himself and not a person determined by structures outside himself. He was gradually discovering what he specifically had to give as a leader, and, without having all answers already prepared, he began to accept that the particular characteristics of himself, his deeper mind and his heart, might be exactly what was needed from him as a leader. He helped a number of leaders to simply become what they are – human.

When we engage more consciously in voicing and listening, we also develop our capacity to use life's essential feedback mechanism more. Rather than waiting for life to throw our impact back at us, we begin to observe resonance more actively and we ask for feedback. This engagement in a feedback cycle can be scary. Feedback challenges our identity. Thus our ability to open to feedback is very closely linked to the way we handle our identity. The more tightly we hold onto it, the less we will ask for feedback or take it into consideration when it comes our way.

We might lack the capacity to integrate feedback (which we always assume will be negative) into our internal developmental process. We keep defending the structure of identity that is containing us, or, at least, that we believe is containing us. We might be afraid of feedback that may dismantle the image we have of ourselves, or we might be so convinced of our way of being and participating in the world that feedback *per se* does not have much relevance for us. Or we operate at the other end of the spectrum. The less sure we are about our identity, the more we might interpret any resonance from others as feedback guiding us onto a road to nowhere – we get lost listening to the voices of others more than we listen to our own. Neither of these ways of participating in the natural feedback process of life really helps us to find our way home.

A Glimpse into Theory: The Construction of Inner and Outer Worlds

The Chilean neuroscientist Humberto Maturana, together with biologist Francisco Varela, developed the concept of self-organization or autopoiesis (Maturana & Varela, 1987) as an organizational feature common to all living systems: the components of a living system are not stable, they continuously transform or 'make themselves.' This process of 'making themselves' does not happen independently from the whole. Each transformation reflects a transformation in the relationship environment. In this way, components enter into a process of 'making' each other as well, and so the entire network constantly 'makes itself' – a continual and eternal feedback process in a vast network. One of the most revolutionary aspects of this theory is the concept of cognition it implies, known as the Santiago Theory of Cognition (Capra, 1996; Varela, Thompson & Rosch, 1991). The central insight is identifying cognition, the process of knowing, with the process of life itself. Cognition, according to Maturana and Varela, is the activity involved in the self-generation and self-perpetuation of all living systems (Varela et al.; 1991; Capra, 1996, 2003). In other words, cognition is the very process of life creation. It embraces perception, emotion, and behaviour – and does not necessarily require a brain and a nervous system.

At the human level, however, cognition includes language, conceptual thought and all the other attributes of human consciousness. In the Santiago theory of cognition, mind and matter no longer appear to belong to two separate categories, but are seen as representing two complementary aspects of the phenomenon of life. At all levels of life, beginning with the simplest cell, mind and matter, process and structure are inseparably connected. This becomes quite apparent in the way the theory handles the old question of the relationship between the mind and the brain, which is seen as a relationship between process and structure (Capra, 1996). Cognition is no longer seen as the representation of an objective, independently existing, world (Bateson, 2000). There is no world 'out there' independent from the process of cognition (Varela, Thompson & Rosch, 1991). Cognition creates the world and the world sets a frame for cognition: an eternal feedback loop of creation.

When one looks at the developmental path of a leader through the lens of the Santiago theory of cognition, it presents an enormous challenge because it contradicts our habitual way of seeing the world as independent from us. But the new concept of cognition, as we have seen, is conceptualized not as a process of representation of outside events and objects (Bateson, 2000), but as a process of 'bringing forth of the world' (Capra, 1996, p. 270) in the co-creation of endless feedback processes. It distinguishes between two different processes as a result of cognition. One is *cyclical* change, describing the constant change of a system with the aim or result of maintaining its stability. This process of maintenance could be understood as a process ensuring a system's coherence and identity. The other is *structural* change: as a function of its structure, a system responds to perturbations with developmental change. New structures emerge, new connections are established and the system's overall structure and organization slowly or rapidly change. Both kinds of change are going on all the time, ensuring the system's survival.

If we take this idea into consideration in understanding our leadership journey, it enables us to reconcile with the intertwined aspects of preserving and, at the same time, developing our identity. Life is not something developing independently from us, to which we can react. We simply participate in this unending process of feedback and can do so more or less consciously, with more or less attention. Hence, our identity is not given to us – it is not an internal structure we are called on to maintain, but an ever-fluid process of change and integration of feedback. Yet with all feedback we are willing to take on we will still integrate it into a relatively stable structure: our identity – different from others. What we bring forth in the world is a unique composition of our particular structure of identity (mind and body) in response to the world – the feedback coming to us. 'What is brought forward by a particular organism in the process of living is not *the* world but *a* world, one that is always dependent upon the organism's structure' (Capra, 1996, p. 270). The world, then, does exist, objects are perceivable, but, neither can one organism (or one person) perceive reality in the same way another person would perceive it, nor is the reality around us independent of the constant process of its collective construction through our cognition. Past structure determines how cognition takes place and with what kind of results. We are captives of our past choices and subsequent structures created, and at the same time, we are free to choose anew from the vast array of possibilities every day. Both aspects are true. The way we integrate feedback will change the structure of our identity. In turn, the new form of structure will determine our way of cognizing. Although structure determines, it does not do so in a predictable way – rather, it channels the possibilities without clearly determining what will be the outcome of conscious choice.

'... When a living system reaches a bifurcation point, ... its history of structural coupling will determine the new pathways that become available, but which pathway the system will take remains unpredictable' (Capra, 1996, p. 221). A structurally coupled system can thus be seen as a learning system (Capra, 1996, p. 219), based on a continuous feedback process, and its movement as a developmental path. If I incorporate this into my thinking about leaders' developmental pathways, it could imply that the more feedback processes are made conscious, or actively invited, the more the person will be able to learn and open to learning – that is, to bring forth new forms of structural coupling with the environment and to allow structural changes within.

Different people, of course, change differently, and over time each person forms a unique, individual pathway of learning in the process of personal development. Since the developmental path of a leader is determined by choice, the level of awareness about one's process of taking in feedback is crucial for the way in which re-organizing one's identity takes place.

Our identity is constantly changing as a result of feedback, solicited or not, and yet our identity maintains overall stability. Our developmental path as a leader can be understood as a constant inner change and reconstruction while creating, maintaining and further developing an overall identity. Nothing is fixed, and yet all inner and outer development is influenced by the combination of mind and structure that preceded the new development. We are captive to our own internal mental and physical structure, and yet we are the constant co-creators of this very structure. There is utmost opportunity for free will to change, and at the same time there is utmost limitation: our mental and constitutional structures determine the range of possibilities for change. The more rigidly we hold the structure of our identity, the fewer the choices available to us. We might be able to avoid or ignore crises, but we are less likely able to integrate disturbing experiences. The freedom to change ourselves as a result of experience and the integration of feedback is limited to a certain degree by our embodied memory – the historic structure of our identity limits the pathways we can take. Yet the ability to see anew, to cognize in a different way, is always available to us and can induce different structural changes as a result of it. Freedom exists and choice is possible.

Like a circular path, voicing yourself in the sense of reconnecting with your deeper values, listening to yourself and others with an open heart and integrating feedback more consciously could increase your range of choices. The structure of your identity is maintained in its core, yet becomes flexible enough to integrate both inspiring and disturbing experiences. Seeing the developmental path of a leader through the lens of life's evolutionary feedback process nourishes a deeper serenity: developing as a leader is much less a constant struggle of self-improvement and outer performance than it is an increasingly conscious participation in this dance of life. No one can know quite whose choreography the dance follows, but, with a gradually increasing level of awareness, reflection and listening, with an openness to discover what has not been seen before, we can join the dance in a different, more intense way, and participate in changing the pattern and movements of the dance in collaboration with other dancers. The developmental path of a leader is not, after all, a constant focus on the development of the self and a preconceived image of one's future identity, but the growing capability to be in the world more consciously, more able to participate mindfully, and with less danger of blocking our own or another's process of unfoldment.

We might begin the journey of coming home by enjoying our place in the universe. I believe that more conscious participation in collective co-creation, and a growing awareness about the way our minds operate in perceiving the world and responding to it, is a prerequisite for leading in favour of life and humanity. It opens a new gateway – we gradually begin to listen to a larger whole.

Diane grew up in Europe with an American mother and an Italian father. She was very conscious of the cross-cultural issues in her own home. Her deeper earlier intention had always revolved around integration. One of her earliest childhood dreams was to adopt disadvantaged children. Another was getting money from the rich or making large amounts of money and giving it to the poor:

> I was deeply aware, from a very young age, of how fortunate I was to have been born into a family that was financially secure. And that only fate had kept me from being born into a poor family. I do remember loving stories such as Robin Hood where the hero robs from the unfeeling rich to give to the poor. I [have] never really lost the dreams completely.

As a high school student, Diane was fascinated with anthropology and the variety of cultural expressions of the world's different tribes, groups, and subcultures. It was very clear that she wanted to understand the differences in order to connect to the underlying similarities:

> I don't know if I was clear on what all this study was going to enable me to become in terms of a profession or calling, but I do remember thinking that what I didn't want to become was someone who was under the illusion that there was only one right way of doing things. I wanted to know the range of differences of experiences that existed for people of different cultures in order to bridge those differences and connect with what is essentially, at the very core, human. And I came to clarify my belief that essentially, at the very core, true human-to-human connection is about connecting, however fleetingly, the spirit that lives within each of us. It is about seeing past the hypnotically beautiful variety of cultural expressions, to the fundamental patterns that are shared.

After high school and university, Diane made her career in a multinational energy company and held a number of different leadership positions. When she turned forty, she felt that she had arrived at a point in her leadership journey where she needed time to reflect rather than quickly to move on to the next challenging assignment:

CHAPTER TWO: PARTICIPATION

> At this moment in my life I actually need to stay very still and wait to see what emerges and then move in that direction, without giving it too much weight by deciding it is all or nothing. I am starting to become much more conscious of my own ability to influence and lead or not to influence and lead. I am becoming aware of the difficult manifestations of my leadership journey. Sometimes I feel trapped by either wanting to lead maturely or moving back into a state of lack of responsibility. It is still casting and experimenting. I am starting to have moments of insights into my voice – if I step back I can actually see how much power I do yield and how much I influence. But there are moments when I lose track of why I am doing certain things; it is more the adrenalin rush of having been successful or having had the influence of controlling certain events; and it is rather the intoxication of being power manic; and then I notice that all of a sudden I have let myself lose the centre. But I think at this moment in my life, being true to myself is more important than having access to power or the impression that I have access to power, or to appease other people's dreams for me. It is about being true to my core.

Diane noticed that she gradually felt she became more accountable to people or groups within her organization who didn't have a voice, or who were not being heard. She began to mentor younger women in her organization. She finally moved jobs and started a leadership position centred on inclusion and diversity:

> This is my conscious choice, because it is about wanting to contribute to the organization so that more voices can be heard. I always had the belief that at the very core of every person is this very pure untouched light and that we are all

CHAPTER TWO: PARTICIPATION

actually trying to constantly connect with that both in ourselves and in others. And that's why we have this human need for connection. In myself it has manifested itself as a passion for eliminating the injustices or lack of authority around people's ability to be themselves, it is the inherent freedom that everyone should have. This is actually what informs my journey, and it is kind of strange to connect back with the history of my values. I actually enjoy leading now through allowing others to take up their leadership.

The creative process of leading takes place in a balanced relationship between the emergence of our own voice and vision, and our increasing ability to listen to and observe our own transformative process, as well as that of others travelling with us. Both individual and collective reflection can facilitate our move into more conscious co-creation. Finding, developing and speaking our voice is paramount, but awareness of the co-creative process shifts our sense of self away from the idea of 'self-actualization' as a goal in itself and towards an intentional participation in the process of creative unfolding in collaboration with others. If we avoid participating over a longer period of time, if what we do is a far cry from our deeper intention and bears little relation to our quest, our source of energy and creativity dwindles. Leading as a creative process requires listening as an act of responsiveness to what we perceive to be needed in the world. As we loosen the boundaries of our self-sustaining identity and let the humanity of other people touch our hearts, we also begin to perceive a larger story of which we are part. We begin to listen to the whole. Even the most outward goal to achieve, the most difficult problem to solve or element to influence starts with an inner journey. Understanding ourselves precedes our understanding of others. We experience less theoretically and more experientially the fact that the Universe is a web of relationships, in which nothing comes into being by the intention or willpower of a single person. Even though we know little about how the process of co-creation happens in our daily lives, this insight leads to greater humility and a greater feeling of responsibility. We engage with the present in a different way. Before we start looking for a connection to the whole, we need to reconnect with our own deeper intention, the history of our voice and our values.

It might be helpful not to see our own leadership journey as linear, but to imagine it as a spiral movement, a movement inseparable from the underlying holo-movement of the evolutionary process, which we can grasp theoretically but rarely experience. I see it as a spiral movement because a spiral combines recurrence and innovation. Movements take place in a similar shape, around a centre and in relation to the previous movements but on a different level. How much of it is our choice, how much we do steer this process, how much of our transformation is an unconscious reaction to influences outside ourselves, and how much is determined by something other than us, we cannot know for sure. We can't escape the dilemma between free will and determinism on our leadership journey. Our actions, both from conscious choices and those that are more unconscious reactions, intervene in a dynamic field of existing-but-constantly-changing manifest reality, and into existing-but-constantly-evolving structures in co-action with others, who also intervene. It is almost like a billiards table, with balls already moving in all directions into which we bring the force of yet another ball. The path the ball will take depend on its own force and direction, but is also heavily determined by the collisions with other balls. Steering and collision, choice and determinacy, are inextricably linked. We learn, are inspired, have new revelations and meet new opportunities as we collide with or encounter people, structures, events, experiences. Determinism and free will coexist and develop together.

There is a red thread running through our leadership journey,

CHAPTER TWO: PARTICIPATION

which I believe we can track back to our early journey – we hold something at our core that, even though it might get pushed into the background, holds our inner reality, a deeper intention and the seeds for our form of participation in the world. Every moment is an invitation to open a new doorway, move in a new direction, develop a new variation of the theme; nothing is ever fixed once and for all. But it is turning around a central core, a central theme. I believe that this central theme makes itself known when centrifugal forces take us too far away from it. This happens in many variations, at all ages, at different points on our leadership journey.

For Gerard, it happened most profoundly in his late thirties when he finally decided to leave the multinational company and take one year off before engaging in another organization. The theme of his early journey surfaced as he moved back to his home region in France, a place surrounded by mountains and vivid nature:

> Where I am right now is that, all of a sudden, rereading some notes here and there, the word that keeps coming into to my mind is 'harmony'. I realize that I never paid attention or actually cared about harmony around me, maybe in a family setting, but definitely not in a business setting. Where I am now on the journey is realizing as an individual and as a leader that working on the harmony of the thing, also in an organizational setting, is important.

For Mandy it was her fiftieth birthday that marked a point of reflection:

> I just turned fifty last year, and I have felt I knew I was at a kind of turning point or inflection point where I would be needing to make choices that had always been nagging at me, now that there is the time to make choices and take

a real step into having more of a voice in the world than I have ever allowed myself to have, like beginning to trust in my own competence, into myself as a woman and not as a disintegrated person, whose sensuality and sense of sexuality were somehow fragmented and disengaged from the whole. What is it that I want to say as a leader and what stand do I want to take? And that question remains open.

The rhythm of the spiral movement is particular to each of us, with outside events accompanying and facilitating a process of inner evolution. How this transformation takes place for us is also a function of our very particular relationship with change. We all have our own conscious model of change – this is what we apply when we lead and need to influence people, structures and outcomes. But for ourselves we might not be very aware of how change is happening, both within us and in the way we act. I believe this next step in the archeology of your own leadership journey is a valuable exercise. How does change happen for me? What causes me to change within? Some experiences trigger changes more than others, and although there cannot be one model of change, there seems to be an underlying consistency that change within needs a resonance between something happening outside and a place within ourselves that recognizes this moment as significant. Dissatisfaction can be the cause as much as sudden insights, relationship encounters, a sudden attraction, or a gradually growing awareness that life needs to take a different direction.

There are many changes of direction on a leader's journey, not all of which touch our hearts. They can be caused by serious crises or fast decisions. Not every change outside leads to a change within or to a deeper inquiry. *The crucial moment occurs when we become aware of our identity changing, when we notice we need to integrate and transcend experience.*

Reflections

Can you remember the history of your voice? How did it begin? How do you make yourself heard?

What would a leader you were willing to follow voluntarily be like?

How does change within happen for you?

What is your relationship to feedback?

Chapter 2: Summary

- Leading is a form of participation in the dance of life that differs from not-leading. We need to become aware of our impact and responsibility as nodes in a network co-enacting reality.
- At the core of life-enhancing leadership is the ability to respect human beings as human beings, acknowledge difference, and integrate diversity.
- It is therefore helpful to review our participation in the emergence of reality – do we shy away from contributing? Do we feel urged to determine outcomes? How do we contribute to mutual consistency?
- If we attend to the whole more consciously, we notice that it too needs expression, but we cannot think on behalf of it. We need to ask. Participation and inclusion is thus the best way to give the whole its legitimate voice.
- When we begin to communicate more consciously, it can be helpful to reconstruct the history of our own voice. Finding and expressing our real voice might be a slow process, but it becomes essential to the re-definition of our leadership journey.
- When we have tracked the history of our voice, we begin to listen in a different way. This can encourage us to invite feedback more actively, an important feature for developing the learning identity that sustainability leadership needs.
- The creative process of leading takes place in a balanced relationship between the emergence of our own voice and vision and our increasing ability to listen to and observe our own transformative process and that of others travelling with us. Both individual and collective reflection can facilitate our move into more conscious co-creation.

CHAPTER THREE
COHERENCE

Many of the changes we go through on our leadership journey are the result of relatively fast decisions, geared to keep the journey going and informed by the rationale of our career path. We react and act. Rarely do we sit back for any length of time and let experiences, thoughts and feelings sink in; rarely do we allow ourselves to *not* have an answer and let our experience ferment so that we can gradually transform and mature into who we are at our core. If we have created good personal relationships, we might at times contemplate changes together with our spouse or friends. It is extremely helpful to be able to have this one-on-one dialogue with another person. For some of us, the only opportunity for this might be through a coach.

Even less frequently do we talk about our inner and outer changes in a collective setting among leaders. The organizations most of us work in may pay lip service to it, but don't really support this type of collective reflection. This is sad, because as human beings, we are children of language. Not exclusively, but to a great extent, we transform through encounter and conversation. Transcendence is supported by thinking together with others. Change on a deeper level can be facilitated by mutually respectful dialogues. The more we can feel at home in a respectful feedback network of life, the greater our chance *not* to block experience and, especially when it is negative, to lock it in a lost corner of our mind. We can more readily welcome the essence of learning in it. Life is about constant change, yet the crucial point on a leader's journey seems to be the moment when change becomes conscious and so is not simply reacted to or carried out. If the urge to change something is accompanied by the space and time that an inquiry into one's journey requires, the quality of the change can be different – it can reach a new depth, become more profound. This might be the case when reflection has yielded the recognition of certain patterns or streams of experience. Viewing experience and action from the outside can help us to let go of habitual ways of doing or avoiding things. Change is inevitable – the only influence we have is on *how we become its partner*. But more often we resist change – not the changes we ourselves create but the ones we encounter and have little influence over. We do reach points where experiences cannot just be accepted on face value and simply integrated into life. Also, the helpful explanations and subsequent reactions of the past might no longer be appropriate to the circumstance or who we have become. The point where reflection brings about questions that cannot be answered immediately is the moment when stillness and space become more important than anything else. Paradoxically, in the stillness we begin to move closer to the 'edge of chaos'. We are less likely to ignore disarray and we sense the early signs of a deeper transformation.

Conscious change usually begins when our heart becomes involved and when we allow the stillness more often. This is always accompanied by questions. For a leader, a process of transformation that is likely to access the deeper aspects of our humanity in leading will involve a more conscious experience of the internal, and, subsequently, the external change process. There is a rhythm of transformation that is particular to us and no two rhythms are the same. Understanding our leadership journey and redefining our contribution require that we understand our transformational patterns on a deeper level.

A Glimpse into Theory: Change of Living Systems

As do smaller entities, larger systems evolve slowly over time, apart from the occasional sudden change that might be fast and unexpected. With the concept of the two types of change, cyclical and developmental change, in mind (Capra, 1996, p. 218 and 219), we can understand evolution as a 'creative unfolding of life in forms of ever-increasing diversity and complexity' (Capra, 1996, p. 222). Rather than seeing evolution as a process of random mutations that are then selected on the basis of strength and for the sake of adaptation to a seemingly independent environment, living systems theory suggests that both kinds of change happen all the time. In this way life creates its environment and vice versa. Even though this process is constantly striving for balance and harmony, it never reaches complete harmony. A state of temporary harmony is always followed by imbalance and new search for harmony. 'If nature reached perfection, its evolution would come to a stop.' (Sahtouris & Lovelock, 2000, p. 223). Mutual consistency is the result of constant change, continual development and an ongoing process of balancing. This requires a high degree of creativity. In such continuous evolution, the maintenance of a system's identity is a temporary state of balance in the constant flux of systems.

Reality *is* change, and we, like everything else, are participants in this 'dance of change'. However, as human beings we can become aware of outer and inner change and influence our participation in the dance. When you begin to unearth your own patterns of transformation, you will find the gradual change over time and the change as a result of sudden insight, experience or encounter. You will find processes of slowly growing into a new identity and you will find sudden forces of change that leave you surprised at their impact. You will also find yourself changing reactively to events happening in the world that have an impact on you. When you chart the memories of your past, you will find what you did and did not do, what helped and what did not help to integrate these experiences so that you could be at ease with what happened. Or you might discover that you are still carrying leftovers from forced changes that you could not integrate, in such a way that you feel reconciled with them. You will, on the other hand, find changes that were a result of your conscious and rational choices, deliberate re-directions of your life, adventures into new areas, confrontations with challenges that you welcomed.

You might find a third quality of change, moments of insight when something in your heart changed and you knew that you would change directions without being able to trace all the threads of cause and effect. Often the intuitive understanding of *resonance* is an important factor for change within. Internal change on our leadership journey is not necessarily rational, but often a very intuitive and emotional process. If something inside us resonates with something we heard, encountered, or experienced, a new pathway opens up. A field of change occurs – the fertile ground for maturation.

When Gerard had time to reflect on his leadership journey during his one-year sabbatical, he became aware of the history of events, internal reactions and insights that mapped the path to where he was:

> You don't decide to change. You do not wake up one day and decide to do something different, for whatever reason, and then do it – that's not sufficient. Change within needs to resonate, there is a need for a spark to come from somewhere that we didn't think about initially, or it might be a piece of information one has completely disregarded and then it comes back. So it comes essentially from the environment. Something resonates with something deep inside me. Once that resonance has been established there is the desire for change.

CHAPTER THREE: COHERENCE

So, it is not myself independent from the environment, and it is not the environment changing without me. They are both integrated and where there is resonance there is impact.

I believe that this resonance is more than just chance. Transformative change, the kind of change within that brings us closer to ourselves, and closer to our feeling of being at home in the Universe, is based on a resonance with something that is already in us. It might have been dormant and in need of revival. It is a deeper core of our identity. It might be the quest reminding us of our path, or deeper values pushing their way to the surface. When we change within we do not re-invent ourselves, although it might look like it on the surface because it can result in changing career, home and relationships. We essentially reconnect with who we are in our essence.

Evolution is always open to change, but never breaks with the past. Nature always guarantees continuity – even through vast periods of chaos and instability. When we change we also remain faithful to the past – not to all aspects of it, but to our deeper quest. The core is maintained throughout the journey. When we let go, voluntarily or not, and enter inner transformation, we also let go of images of our identity while staying faithful to our knowledge from the heart, a deeper knowing that will never be completely lost. This knowing connects the phases of our journey throughout all our encounters and experiences. Where once it manifested as a deeper early intention, now it has matured in the fire of life's melting pot. Even if we aren't always aware of it, evolution has an overall pattern of harmony and 'holding together' throughout the process of disintegration and re-integration. We are part of this. There is our unique storyline, the centre of the spiral. We are structured by experience yet we always have choices, one of which is to choose how we respond.

After Samson left his lecturing post at the university, he and colleagues established a business college in Ethiopia. He played a central role, greatly inspired by his values and the inner driving force to prove that it was possible to set up an educational institution in line with those values. This was very important in maintaining his emotional balance and not feeling defeated after resigning from his lecturing post. His search continued. When he began to reflect on the way inner transformation happened for him, he saw the central theme as the need for freedom of choice as a catalyst for deeper change:

> If any deeper change has happened in me it was through what I call 'self-talk'. It could be that I was reading something or I had been listening to a speech or I found something – the resonance with it would bring about change. That's how I found myself changing. What I don't respond to is pressure – consistently I find myself blocking when it comes to outside pressure of power or force. But when I am relaxed, ideas can resonate in me, something I encounter clicks, so that is what I have in mind when I say self-talk.

We are relaxed when we feel no need to defend the image we have of ourselves. We relax when we begin to accept ourselves the way we are – with all our patterns, limitations, dreams, quests, potentials, capabilities and inabilities. If you begin to track the patterns of your leadership journey, re-connect with your quest and think about re-defining your leadership contribution, you do not need to acquire new skills. Keep what you've acquired so far and be open to new learning, but for the purposes of reconnecting with your deeper intention and redefining your leadership contribution, you can just be you the way you are. Deeper change does not take place intellectually. If our heart resonates with an outer encounter, we're one step closer to home. This resonates because it is familiar. We might not have been aware of it, but something resonates because we have known it all along without having been able to express it and without having been taught it or told it. Or it resonates when we tap into a deeper knowledge that we all have access to because we are human. Mind and heart work together when we change as a result of resonance. We can come home. When we change as a result of resonance, we are voluntarily participating in the great feedback network of life.

Mandy's leadership journey emerged in a mix between her learning to bring out her voice more strongly, her deepest values of participation and acknowledgement for diversity and her career inviting her to operate in a variety of tough business settings with people who don't necessarily hold the same values. When she reflected on change, what came into focus in her memory was the interconnectedness of inner change with people she related to:

> I believe that change happens in relationship and therefore the notion that we can separate ourselves from the relationships we are in has never made sense to me. The way change happens for me is that there are a series of external catalysts that create some kind of response in me. Usually it is a sense of dissatisfaction that seems to be creating a loop between my internal frame of myself and the external catalyst, whatever that might be. Often it is a loop that I cannot continue with. It is not always something bad happening or something I don't like, but it has always to do with somebody else, it is in a relationship or with a group of people. That then generates the question or a challenge to my own thinking. I will usually stand in that loop for quite some time and it will prompt internal reflection. I can hold this until the lack of cohesion between what is going on internally and what I am doing externally becomes irreconcilable. And then I have to

change. I can think of times when what I held internally as an aspiration, externally I did not pursue and that created the kind of loop that I am describing. It is this disequilibrium between the internal and the external world in me that creates change.

We change within when we have opened up to resonance, when we do not defend a rigid image of our identity and when we welcome catalysts for change in the form of people or encounters. We are most likely to change at the edge of chaos and not in the middle of our most harmonious phases. Even though life seems to strive for harmony, it never reaches perfect harmony and it creates constant movement between temporary stability and temporary instability. Life's inherent tendency for creative unfolding into forms of increasing diversity and complexity requires times of stability and times of instability. We are part of this unfolding. The more we accept ourselves and the more diversity we allow within ourselves, the less rigid is our identity. We do fail and we do succeed, we are successful and we are not. We are capable and we are not. As we reconcile with our internal turmoil and accept both happiness and depression as temporary phases on our leadership journey, we become more vulnerable and more responsive. Our capacity to become a partner to change increases.

A Glimpse into Theory: At the Edge of Chaos

The higher internally organized and externally interrelated a living system becomes, the less stable and predictable it becomes (Macy, 1991a, p. 85). It increases its ability to be responsive, to adapt, but it also becomes more vulnerable:
  'This gain in adaptability is won at the cost of structural

stability and imperturbability, as the system becomes more open and susceptible to its environment. In order to register and respond to what is going on, the system becomes more vulnerable. This vulnerability in turn ... enhances its capacity to cope ... For the cognitive system the ability to cope involves adaptation, not just to things as they are, but as they are coming to be. To ensure intelligibility as well as survival, the system seeks to comprehend not only the results of changes, but the factors of change in themselves. Like the tightrope walker who must raise her eyes to keep her balance, the system maintains its dynamic equilibrium by looking ahead. It keeps its balance not by standing still, subsiding into stasis, but by moving forward, projecting its constructs into the future. Such adaptation is a predictive and extrapolative activity, rather than an adjustment to present givens.' (Macy, 1991a, p. 85).

What might look like harmony could actually be dynamic equilibrium, subject to constant change, both cyclical and developmental. Stuart Kauffmann proposes that living systems live best in what he calls the 'boundary region near the 'edge of chaos" (Kauffman, 1995; Capra, 1996, p. 204). He suggests that if a system is centred in the area of ordered stability, its ability to handle complexity is very low. If a system has moved into the centre of chaos, it would be too sensitive to even the smallest perturbations to maintain its identity. 'At the edge of chaos', however, a system seems to have the greatest chance of sustainability, because it is best able to adapt, evolve and coordinate complex and flexible behaviour (see Kauffman, 1993; see also Capra, 1996, p. 204.) Or as Paul R. Fleischmann expresses it: 'On the edge of chaos, a system contains enough order for self-perpetuation, and enough complexity to enable new combinations and permutations, new energies and new relationship to bubble up among fixed corridors of precedent... Fertile complexity endures longest at the edge of chaos.' (Fleischmann, 1999, p. 126).

At the edge of chaos rests creative instability in conjunction with sensitive responsiveness. Vulnerability is an essential part of adaptive creativity. Systems, as Ilya Prigogine proposes (Prigogine & Stengers, 1984; Prigogine, 1996) thrive on ambiguity. They survive and create best in the delicate sphere between order and chaos. Self-organizing systems and human beings definitely fall in this category, and are characterized by continuous spontaneous emergence of new structures and new forms of behaviour in open systems that are far from equilibrium with a constant flow of internal and external feedback loops.

If a living system develops more and more rigidity, it has less and less chance of survival. Even if it builds more and more defensive structures, these will be ultimately in vain. Rigidity is not sustainable in the long run. A healthy balance between necessary boundaries as well as states of stability and an adaptive instability and openness to feedback characterizes a sustainable system. If leading takes place as participation in the unfolding of life, and as a conscious contribution to an evolutionary process of mutual consistency, our internal capacity to find our unique pattern between stability and instability, the one that supports our particular journey, is crucial for the way we lead and for the form of contribution we can make to the world. We need to have temporary states of harmony – neglecting this prevents us from integrating experience into our identity. This process of integration and transcendence has probably as much influence on our leadership role as the visible action we take. We can call the process of integrating experience 'learning', not in

CHAPTER THREE: COHERENCE

the sense of acquiring skills but in the sense of developing a new understanding that gradually contributes to a reorganization of the internal set of structures within our identity. In order to make experience meaningful, we develop new constructs that alter the way we see the world, and because we see the world differently, the world itself changes.

When we begin to inquire into our leadership journey, it could be worthwhile to try and understand how these phases of integration and reconstruction happen on that journey.

Mandy found that she was becoming significantly more aware of different ways of looking at the world simply by *not thinking*, by clearing her mind. In retrospect she saw that she had lived a deeply unbalanced life from her mid teens right up to her mid forties. She noticed that contemplation was least natural to her, yet she always knew when there was a need for it, almost like a yearning hunger:

> I can go right back into my childhood memories, probably my earliest memories, when I was about ten, and I can remember needing to sit silently and alone for a long track of time out in nature, because I just needed time to reflect. So when this need arises it is almost impossible to deny it. It is as if I am starved of a mineral in my body, it gets to a point where I cannot turn my back on it. I am never deeply aware of rejecting this, it is just that I don't have a natural inclination to go inside and sit silently, reflect, until this yearning hunger arises. I can see that there might be catalysts from outside prompting me to that hunger, but I actually do see it coming from within. I see when there is a call for balance. Contemplation has the deepest impact on shifting and changing both internal thought patterns and choices I am able to make, so when I am blocked by something serious I always move to

contemplation. I often just find resources in myself that I know that they are here; it is the act of wakening what is within, it is not always some extraordinary new insight. I have done a lot over many years to try and access ways of building this into my life more steadily. But when I learn something new, a technique, I try it for a while and then the stimulation part of life overwhelms me again. The generic pattern is, when I have the yearning hunger, I will move into contemplation quite deeply, but then I allow stimulation to sweep over that focus. I carry some of it with me, but it doesn't get into a balanced way of moving between contemplation and stimulation. I wonder if when I become aware of the impact of persevering with something at my own expense, that that is when I go into contemplation.

We are not trained in contemplation and reflection. It is neither part of the educational systems we went through nor it is part of the organizational setup that most of us work in. Contemplation is for most of us not only extremely private, it is also not formally acknowledged as time well and efficiently spent. As it is not an acknowledged part of our social life (except for the few of us who are either in religious communities or in spiritual circles), each of us has to struggle through the confusing movement of energies between passion, commitment and contemplation more or less without much guidance. But integrating experience into one's growing identity requires reflection and contemplation, phases of stillness, journeys within, identification of patterns – movements supporting the increasing flexibility of our leadership identity.

Diane had just finished a hugely demanding research project at her multinational company, a project that was dear to her heart and deeper intention because it dealt with the company's socio-economic contribution. As with most projects, this demanded most

CHAPTER THREE: COHERENCE

of her attention for a substantial period. It was not a task she could accomplish with a relaxed attitude to work. Time for contemplation was not built in. After completion of the project, doubtful about its resonance and impact in the company, Diane observed herself moving into a different phase:

> I find myself in the current moment more in a phase of repose and reflection with some touches of a light depression. As I ponder why I am in this energy, I can see that over the past 12 months, I have been consciously focusing on the project with a distinct need to perform, and with high levels of commitment and perseverance, because this was critical in achieving results in the path I had set for myself and because external circumstances seemed to be testing me, and therefore requiring that energy. In the process, I may have under-focused on reflection, and so now that a certain phase or rhythm has ended, I find myself rebalancing the cycle by plunging into that energy both in its generative and its pathological aspects.

Reflection always finds us, whether it is Mandy's yearning hunger for stillness or Diane's move into slightly disenchanted reflection. There is nothing wrong with it. It is a circle turning and helping us to make sense of experience; helping us, in some cases, to re-connect with what we really want, with the core of our intention, with new possibilities for our contribution, with our leadership quest. It often arrives unannounced and we don't always welcome it. It is worth tracking the movement between action and reflection through life thus far. If we neglect the energy needed to ease the fermenting and integration of experience, it will find its way back to us. It is like a voice that calls to us. The difficult task is to welcome it when it arrives. We tend to expect quick solutions when reflection arrives as depression; we might ignore it at first and might use more activity to paint over it. It helps if we begin to observe, to notice that there is a change of energies, that there is a new movement, a new phase beginning, the next turn of the spiral. This might manifest as exhaustion, as the desire to withdraw, as light depression, or as discontent. It is an act of courage for a leader to embrace this move into chaos. It helps to know that sitting quietly and observing the chaos is a faculty we can learn: it will, sooner or later take us into a new movement of focussed activity.

When Edith moved out of social work into the corporate world, she faced the challenges of her new profession head-on. She started work in the telecommunications industry and progressed quickly in her new career. After a few years, she set up her own company in New York. She enjoyed the speed and stimulation she experienced in driving her own international business. But when she looked back to this period of her life she noticed a serious lack of reflection:

> When I had my business in New York I flew to Germany about once a week. I managed a large group of people and the business was thriving. I was also in a relationship and my partner fell ill with cancer. This was a time when I was driven by both commitment and stimulation. And there was a point when this wore me out. It was extreme. When the time came to innovate – you constantly have to innovate if you want to stay in business – I missed the Internet. I did hire a manager who was supposed to develop it. But I didn't spend enough time with him to put the ideas in front of me, so I missed that part. There was no time to really sit and reflect and let things evolve. I did other things, I was terribly busy. But I should have done more reflection on innovation. I finally sold the business, the timing was good, my perception of trends was always good. But I do see that that lack of reflection changed a lot. After that I always created time for

doing nothing, time to just feel and let things evolve. Now, years later, after having travelled the world, I cherish my time of contemplation and observation.

Our leadership journey is a path with hurdles and straights. It is a continuous re-organization of our identity in participation in and with the world. While we integrate experience, our mind selects and re-organizes memory. New patterns of our identity emerge. Our self is dismantled and re-built invisibly, sometimes more rapidly then we can grasp, sometimes slowly over time. Learning takes place, consciously or unconsciously. It seems not to matter what is 'objectively' taking place, so much as it matters what our perception is making of it. *What our mind does with what has happened determines our future action.* We enter into a more or less conscious learning cycle that is very particular to us – our intention, our quest, our experience, our growing identity. Inquiry and reflection can help us transcend experience. They help create the fertile ground for learning between instability and stability as they alternate in our very personalized pattern. Real learning takes place 'at the edge' of chaos.

The more flexible our frame of identity becomes, the more we are able to integrate life's experience into a larger context. We begin to see other people travelling with us, struggling to make sense of experience, trying to come home. We can see the patterns of others while we reconstruct our own. As we become more aware, we become connected with a larger story. The more we reconcile our own experiences, the more we open up to other people's journeys. We realise that no leader's developmental path can be smooth or linear and free of severe obstacles. Even though we can seldom see this in times of chaos, over time we begin to see that even the wildest disarray is likely to contain some subtle coherence and order. Examined in retrospect, our path becomes coherent. We can integrate experience and find the thread of our journey. We learn that stability is not a state to be finally achieved, not something we need to aspire to. We sense that the only state we can work towards is a delicate balance between stability and instability. When we are in the midst of disarray, it is helpful to remember that what looks disturbing in the moment might turn out to be of great learning, if looked at through a wider lens or at a later stage. Periods of instability can be seen as initiators of learning cycles or reminders of the benefits of being 'at the edge of chaos'. They can appear in different forms – as a crisis, as a perceived failure in life, as a loss of meaning, as misfortune, as inner emptiness, as a new insight, as an emotional disturbance, as an experience of something unfamiliar, or as the desire to withdraw. With a deliberate move into reflection and contemplation, we open the gate to integration.

When we observe experience we notice that times of chaos end – this also changes. We come out stronger. Maturation requires passage through disturbing times of disintegration. In the learning dance between chaos and order our identity's complexity increases, accompanied both by vulnerability and an increasing number of choices. Analogous with nature, flexible stability emerges that manifests in our ability to respond to transformation without endangering our flexible pattern of identity. The relaxation into coming closer to ourselves often results from integrating disturbing experience.

When Paul managed a huge division in a multinational company with as many as 500 people reporting directly to him and a budget worth millions of pounds, he was driven to meet targets and to perform optimally. Then the company merged with another company with similar portfolios. His job was split in two and it dawned on him that this was an opportunity to bring in a lot of new people:

> My boss was moved on, my boss's boss was moved on and I was offered half of what I used to do before and then it struck

CHAPTER THREE: COHERENCE

me that they wanted me to move on as well and that there was nothing I could do about that. When I was possibly at my lowest edge, because I had allowed myself to feel too powerful and therefore thought I can be here forever, when I felt so vulnerable and came within a few weeks of actually wanting to leave the company, it was the first time in my career that I felt I had no choice. Up to that point, I had been exposed to the thinking that you always have a choice. So I wasn't quite mature enough in my thinking to know how to deal with that. What I felt was that I was almost being bullied and controlled by a control freak. That had a huge influence on me, there were some events that shattered my confidence, and made me very anxious as to how I perform in a business context. I recognize that as a turning point in my leadership journey. I felt very powerless.

When we lose our ability to influence we can go through a long period of self-doubt, lack of confidence and an inability to lead with our full potential. Experiences of powerlessness hit our most vulnerable spot, the feeling of not being in control. Powerlessness revives all common fears – the fear of abandonment, failure, betrayal, inadequacy, insignificance, oppression, and loss of control. Although no such crisis on our leadership path is pre-designed, I believe disappointment and disillusionment are an unavoidable part of any leadership journey. However, the feeling of powerlessness can be seen as an initiating experience. When we consider redefining our leadership contribution, the transcendence of experiences of powerlessness is crucial for the way we bring ourselves into the world anew. How we integrate experiences of powerlessness has an impact on the way we learn to handle power. This does not mean that I would recommend deliberately going through states of disappointment, powerlessness and betrayal. But if we can't avoid them, they can become treasures for transformation. How we as leaders relate to both experiences of power and powerlessness has a decisive impact on the growth of our humanness, humility and compassion. As a result, the contribution we are willing to make will change. Experiences of powerlessness confront us with our imperfection and the imperfection of the world. They demand acceptance of reality's complexity – it is not all in our hands, we are part of a greater flow. We are actors and we are recipients. We can develop a greater tolerance towards what we might have perceived as failures, ours and others'. With that comes greater acceptance of other people as they are. We become less judgmental and more inclusive of the disarray of life. But nothing seems to be more difficult than holding an experience of powerlessness as a leader, and simply observing it without judgement. The experience invariably causes a strong and almost unconscious urge to escape and avoid.

Anna, the human resources manager in a large Swedish union was greatly influenced by female role models as leaders in her youth. This helped her to identify herself as a leader very early and with much passion and commitment. She always had the desire to create space for community and togetherness. She did not like to be in situations where she felt either restricted or dominated by male power, yet at the same time she was quite aware that she herself had a tendency to 'bulldoze' or trample on the feelings and boundaries of others when she was convinced of the right path to take. Her experiences of powerlessness were related to her dislike of restricting structures:

> I have felt powerless, in a structural trap, when I am in an organization in a structure that traps me, when I cannot exercise my personal power or the power of my position. When I have encountered that I usually assess quite quickly if there is a chance for me to win. When I realize I could never win,

then I quit. I won't waste my energy. So that is how I handle my feeling of powerlessness. I change the context.

Probably the most common form of dealing with the experience of powerlessness is exactly that – to change the setting, move out, change jobs, do something different. This can be an important milestone on the journey. Even if it is reactive, it can lead to an important transformation. A crisis of powerlessness can initiate an external change that opens up new opportunities. As you track your leadership journey, I believe it is worthwhile remembering your way of reacting to and integrating experiences of lack of power and control.

The reason Edith finally decided to create her own international telecommunications business in New York was a result of an inevitable feeling of powerlessness. She had moved up quickly in another New York-based international company. There she was known for the excellent job she did. But when she expected to move into a more influential position, she was blocked:

> I was up against somebody else being promoted to a higher position I was interested in and I knew it was part of the old boy's network and I hadn't played it as well as the guy. And I really felt angry and powerless about that. There was nothing I could do but deal with it in my way. I left the company and took a better job. This opened the doors to creating my own business. I felt powerless then, but the result, in the end, was that it made me take up new challenges.

If you track your relationship with power and powerlessness, you might come across different patterns. One is to respond to powerlessness with withdrawal. This can result in action leading you further into new realms of your possibilities. It can also push you into a withdrawal of a different kind – disconnection, disengagement and depression. This is the point where transformation of a different kind is needed. When the feeling of powerlessness does not respond to any outer application of change, transcendence of the most disconcerting experiences needs to take place.

Mandy's experience of powerlessness was less related to encounters with structures or people – a feeling of substantial loss of control hit her most when her life was entirely out of balance:

> Sometimes it is as if I am at war with myself. That is when I feel most powerless. I do not experience powerlessness as a result of external forces, because I always see options and I don't feel disempowered. That happens only when I am deeply in battle with myself, when I have lost my way. When this happens I go into depression. It is like a form of denial and giving up.

The feeling of powerlessness is a clear thread running through our development of a sense of self. Not only do our images of self begin to crumble, but also our confidence in our ability to access sources of life energy. The feeling of not being in control can have various degrees of intensity, and our reactions to it are almost always an attempt to regain control of our life in one way or another – through avoidance, leaving, fighting, or consciously reframing the situation. These are all ways of sustaining our sense of self and regaining our lost confidence.

Diane's relationship with the feeling of powerlessness was very much determined by her latent ambivalence towards the environment in which she was working (and performing well) – a highly structured corporate setting:

> Closed power triggers me too easily. I find myself rebelling or getting depressed without even noticing that it is happening.

CHAPTER THREE: COHERENCE

I have had to learn in the past several years how to loosen my connection with the emotions that cause this to happen. How to switch off the memory wiring that makes it happen, and deal as constructively as possible with closed power without falling into the trap of reactive depression.

But if none of the strategies work, there is only one gateway to the transcendence of powerlessness: acceptance. Even when our mind struggles with the reconstruction of our identity in which the experience does not fit, acceptance is the road to take. Acceptance is different from agreement or approval. We seldom agree with what pushed us into the feeling of powerlessness, but we can accept that it is as it is. The result might be a loss of innocence, a touch of sorrow or a period of grief. Invariably, with our capacity to gain distance, we become an observer of our experience. When that happens, the process of transcendence can start, with no marked beginning and no marked end. We might gain important insights from reconstructing the history of our experiences of powerlessness. One insight is that there are situations we cannot undo. We were not in control then, and we are not in control now. We need to accept. Another insight is that obstacles on a road sometimes lead to incredibly creative detours and the possibility to discover areas that we would not have found otherwise, both within and without. If we trace the thread to our identity that is inherent in any experience of powerlessness, in our transcendence of powerlessness we might source new forces of our own creativity.

Steven is a diversity manager at a pharmaceutical company in the United States. His approach to leading has been shaped by his religious upbringing in a very closely knit family. When he was young, he imagined himself having a career in a healing profession. However, he was afraid this would mean too much time away from his family, so he made the more practical decision not to go into medicine. He began to work for a pharmaceutical company. His leadership journey was not an aspiration for grandness and popularity, but very much shaped by the insight into the importance of encounter and empowerment. When he was young, he spent some time in voluntary services in Brazil. This period shaped his love for diversity and his respect for difference. Over the years he found that he needed to redesign his experiences of powerlessness:

> When I have felt powerless, I have found myself falling quickly into disengagement and then depression. Over time I needed to develop my commitment energy in order not to let that immediate reaction of disengaging to occur. I have now learned that through perseverance and engagement, even the most powerless of situations can be turned around. Powerlessness, in the end, is not an objective reality, but a projection of our own insecurities or greed.

Experiences of powerlessness are gateways to deeper perceptions of reality. The most disconcerting experiences sometimes help us to access a deeper sense of life in all its possibilities. When the boundaries of our constructed identity are shaken, and we find a way of integrating the disturbing experience, we transform. We also become more human.

When this happens, we enter into a new feeling of our identity. We depend less on the need to assert our greatness and particularity or to maintain our distinctive separateness from those we have judged negatively. We gain resilience and strength through humor, humility and compassion. What has been dismantled in the periods of instability is being reconstructed into the same person, but with deeper awareness, greater connectedness to life. We become more accepting of life's meandering path and exclude others or unwanted parts of ourselves less. In this time of synthesis it is easier to feel part of a whole. This does not mean that all our questions have been answered at this point or that instabilities, fears and feelings of defeat will be excluded from our journey. But we begin to notice that recurrence is an important feature of our leadership journey. This enables us to regain trust, to know now more profoundly that periods of instability are followed by deeper insights and new levels of trust. Our acceptance of the world *as it is* with all its flaws and all its possibilities for change brings us deeper into life and into humanness.

The experience of powerlessness and eventual transcendence changes the way we lead. It increases our awareness of the role of power in the creation and destruction of life energy. It teaches us about our own need for the nourishment of our sense of self through the feeling of being in control of life's events. It teaches us about our dependency on a certain image of ourselves. And it makes us see how we do not want to be drained of energy. An integrated experience of powerlessness probably contributes to our continuous ability to revive our life energy. But it also cautions our own need to exert power – it will change the way we are conscious of our power and the way we live it in our leadership. We gradually become aware of the patterns behind power and powerlessness.

The experience of holding power and having influence not only sustains our sense of self. It also creates a feeling of being fully alive. It may partly be the superficial awareness of being in control through rendering influence and creating reality according to our wishes, or, more rationally, it may be satisfaction from the achievement of a certain goal, but the actual essence of the experience seems to go beyond that. It appears that experiences of power present themselves as direct access to a very generative life force. When we feel we have the power to change things, the world seems to respond to our self in a fully rewarding way. This creates a feeling of importance, recognition of our presence in the world, and the ultimate acknowledgement of our existence. The enjoyment of power can almost be seen as a substitute for this missing acknowledgement of a person as a person, an ultimate feeling we all yearn for. The more this profound acknowledgement of our existence is lacking in the history of our early journey, the more we might welcome the substitute: acknowledgement through influence. Hence, the experience of power is also a substitute for the feeling of being whole, being fully accepted in the world and being loved that so many of us have craved for so long. It fulfills a deep longing for wholeness. The seduction to power as part of our leadership journey is therefore almost unavoidable. It is bound to happen to a greater or lesser degree. The key to not entering into an addictive relationship with power seems to be awareness, observation and a certain degree of detachment. Sometimes we are made aware of this in the form of a sudden warning, an ephemeral thought, uneasiness, or a feeling of emptiness. The energy boost accompanying the experience of power sustains us, but when we become more aware and have tracked our own history of powerlessness, this warning can become a welcome companion to our leadership endeavor. We can make friends with this silent observer. Some people describe this as a loss of themselves, a sudden realization of the addiction to power or the feeling of hollowness. Others find themselves observing the shift to power addiction in other people and they take this as a reminder.

There is no need to refrain from power. But the gradually increasing awareness of what it does to us and others helps to re-establish a new relationship with power on our leadership journey. It is easier to admit the feeling of powerlessness than to confess that we enjoy being powerful and having influence. But if you are in the process of redefining your leadership journey, you cannot skip this part. Your memory will be much weaker than it was in remembering the feeling of powerlessness. Your self will probably rebel against the need to review your relationship with power as well. What is wrong with it anyway? Nothing. But there is a need for awareness. Power changes the world. The way it is held and handled has an enormous impact on the quality of that change. The history of humankind is evidence of this. It can destroy, cause suffering, extract life energy. It can create, empower, and sustain life. Your self might argue that you do not really hold power anyway. You do. Any of your leadership interactions are also an act of power. You do influence. There is no way out of it. Most of us are ambivalent about power because we have not integrated these two sides of the same coin – our relationship with power and our experiences of powerlessness.

Lucia has changed jobs often in the multinational energy company, given the fact that she spent only three years in the company. When the company bought another similar one, she followed her boss, who was now one of the important merger leaders, into a different country as his personal assistant:

> When I went into my last job, I was rubbing shoulders with power. I was working alongside it, and working with it as opposed to being in a direct chain of command. This changed my relationship with power. I was lucky to see it being exercised in an equitable and fair manner. I was respectful of the way power was exercised, but I wasn't in awe. These managers were powerful in the organization, but I could also see how they worked and how they interacted with other people and suddenly they became human and it changed my relationship with them completely. I did begin to think it was not so inconceivable that I could fill that role one day. That was a strange experience. It really made me think. Have you seen *Lord of the Rings*? The ring is the ring of the rings. It gives you enormous power, but it is also dangerous. There are a couple of really good people who try and help others, but when they see the ring they become intoxicated by the power of the ring.

CHAPTER THREE: COHERENCE

There is a warning. What if I put on the ring, and there is no one to check on me? I enjoy the power of influence when other people listen to me. But in the short time I have worked in this company I have also observed that the more power you have the more stuff you have to protect, whether it be your reputation, your salary, or your territory. You have more to protect as you go up in the company. The stress becomes more apparent and I think it does create a certain amount of paranoia, because the more power you have, the more you want to keep it. I think that can really corrupt people. I have really seen this 'the more to lose' part, because I have seen people making decisions that quite blatantly did not benefit the organization. They lose sight of the whole, the whole disappears for them and they are just subsumed by their own self. It becomes more and more important and I have seen that happen with very senior leaders in my company. I felt really let down by them. It made me wonder if it is worth giving all this time that I could spend in more worthwhile ways being with other people, building a superior world class organization that works as efficiently as possible and makes the world a better place. It is a striking insight when you see very, very good people make a recommendation and then have somebody veto it because it would take away something from his territory. I think addiction to power pushes people into regression, almost as if they go back to the playground.

The paradox is that the feeling of being in power not only nourishes our sense of self and inflates the image of our identity, the addiction to it – like any other addiction – disconnects us from our true self, from our deeper values, our intention, our leadership quest, our humanity. We might achieve the impossible and be rewarded for it in various ways. But we also approach the danger of losing the thread

CHAPTER THREE: COHERENCE

of our journey. The insidious way this happens makes it difficult to understand the thin line between power and service, between the superficial feeling of being whole as a result of the potency of our influence and the deeply connected feeling of being whole as a result of being in service to the common good from the heart. The latter stems from the wish to contribute and is nourished by a deeper serenity towards life and the acceptance that we are part of a larger whole that needs expression.

Diane often moved between the world of her dreams, in which people care about meaning and connectedness, and the thrill experienced from the pace of the power-driven organizational culture she worked in:

> In the middle of my own weakness of enjoying the feeling of power and influence, I notice that I am ambivalent towards power, but perhaps because I equate power automatically with closed power (as in command and control). My concern is that power can be misused. I warn about closed power and also influence, if entered into carelessly – the concern that through lack of self-awareness or simply unawareness, I could damage someone else's sense of self.

Paul spent nearly thirty years in the same multinational company, has held many different leadership positions and, in the last couple of years, has enjoyed his human resource position as a way of giving back the rich experiences of his leadership journey to the company:

> I was attracted to power and what attracted me to power was being in a position of authority, being in control and having a say in how things move. I liked the power position in the traditional business hierarchy. If I look back on it, it didn't

feel quite right, but I would not have been able to answer why. So there was a warning, easy to ignore. Power to me now is more an internal sense of attunement. I still I enjoy power of influence but more in the way that I can see the value I can bring to any particular situation, to other people, be it at work or at home in the family.

We cannot avoid being seduced by power on our leadership journey. It will happen again and again. But we can track our history of it and thus become gradually more aware of when and how it happens, what the result is, and how our path continues. We can also voluntarily ask for feedback. There are ways of integrating our relationship with power into our intention to redefine our leadership contribution. Transcending the seduction of power, maintaining one's centre in the midst of the attraction to power, being able to feel fully alive without the need to build our self through exertion of power, contributing to the world without the need for making the world dance to our tune – these are recurrent challenges on a leader's journey. The key is not to avoid situations of power and influence, not to disown one's ability to be influential, but to constantly re-establish the link to one's inner core and to continually ask 'how do I contribute?'

The deeper initial intention, the quest, the unearthing of our voice, the discovery of our transformation patterns, the realization of our attraction to power and the experience of powerlessness are all links to the thread of our leadership journey. When you begin to track the history of all these aspects of your journey you have charted part of the inner territory of leading. You can see in retrospect that changes without and within are connected. You become more in tune with the silent observer of your own journey who regularly reminds you what this is all about. Again, there are no final answers and neither are there recipes. But in tracking your history you have

CHAPTER THREE: COHERENCE

begun to reorganize your memory and subsequently your identity. You become more open to your own humanity. And you cannot avoid opening up to other people's humanity. When this process starts, healing and integration have taken root. You are not only integrating your own experiences, you see yourself integrating into a larger story that reaches beyond the bounds of your own personal story. The process of healing can be seen as a process of overcoming a fragmented sense of self and of being able to experience the world and ourselves as inseparable. As you move towards deeper serenity built on the ground of compassion, your leadership journey is likely to change.

Our capacity to handle crises and our ability to open up to their potential facilitate the transition to the next cycle in our journey's spiral. To become more aware of how and when this happens is probably the most crucial step in being able to redefine our contribution. We pass through different fields and phases, each with its own characteristics. Whether through crisis or insight, the transition from one field to the next is marked by the capacity to learn and integrate experience in a constant movement between stability and instability. This happens in a unique way for each of us. So, too, the velocity with which the spiral turns and the path it takes are different for each of us.

Bearing in mind that there are no recipes and leadership pathways are diverse I would like to suggest a model that could support you in understanding the ebbs and flows and your own experience of disarray. This model may not be true for all of us, but if it serves to clarify an otherwise misty area for you, I would be delighted. Even if it does not speak to you, you may take it as an invitation to observe.

The model goes back to the ideas of Otto Scharmer (2000) whose ability to describe life's deeper movements in easily understandable diagrams I really admire. It has inspired my thinking and what

I'm presenting here is an integration of my own experience into the original model. Although diagrams are two-dimensional and cannot fully describe reality, they can be used to extract and enlarge aspects of reality, which can help you map your own path between chaos and order on your leadership journey. See it as a cycle we go through, and not as suggesting an equal speed for all of us.

In this proposed model there is a *first field* that is one of order in relative stability (see page 246). When we are here the structure of our identity is predominantly unchallenged; we know how things are or how they have to be. The world is familiar, we know where to go and we have a clear image of who we are. We don't think or reflect a lot, disturbances can be pushed aside. They can be reframed or ignored. Experiences are integrated into pre-existing structures in our memory. We might spend a long time in this field or we might only experience this for a short period of time. This depends on our unique journey.

We are moved out of this stable state by the kind of disturbances that cannot be integrated, denied or pushed aside. These disturbances can be experienced as uneasiness, emotional turmoil, failure, disconnection or a deeper crisis. Our first reaction is often denial, the second defence. We want the stable state to be permanent. The irritation causes discomfort, and we have a tendency to hold on to the phase of stability. Only when we cannot avoid accepting the crisis as it is do we move into a second field.

The *second field* is characterized by internal disarray and often differing, or even contradictory and inconsistent, inner voices. Often it is accompanied by a feeling of shame or a sense of failure. We are approaching chaos. We notice the incoherence in our life and feel the inner disorder. This is extremely uncomfortable. If holding on to our previous state of stability is no longer an option, a search begins. We are dissatisfied with ourselves and the world. Fears and insecurities surface and the previous experience of the familiar seems lost to us. The internal chaos emerges to a greater or lesser degree. What was once familiar and clear disintegrates.

We are moved out of this field by our ability to gradually detach from what is happening (inside or outside) and simply observe. The *third field* is one in which our search for understanding and meaning intensifies. At this point, different kinds of questions surface and a deeper inquiry begins. Questions provide hints about directions, but they cannot be answered immediately. Our search becomes more conscious. Attachment to the previous state of stability slowly disappears and we open up to the potential of seeing ourselves and the world in a new way. Our connection to a larger story emerging might become more visible in this phase. Slowly, coherence and understanding emerge as we begin to see the meaning in incoherent experience. Our memory is reorganized when we begin to suspend our old patterns of thinking. Gradually a new order begins to surface. We gain the ability to embrace uncertainty rather than fight it. When we have come through the worst, we might even begin to enjoy the state of reflective instability. Everything seems possible. We view the crisis in a different way and deeper acceptance of unpredictability develops. We prepare ourselves to venture into the unknown.

We move into the *fourth field* when two factors occur. One is our willingness to see and try out new possibilities of both understanding the world and acting in it. The second is the cultivation of our ability to wait for clarity rather than force it. Our vision, and with it our future possibilities, emerge less from an act of will and a need to sustain our identity, than from a growing willingness to contribute and serve. This field is characterized by reflective stability, a state of the mind in which we can allow a diversity of experience to happen without restricting our perceptive capacity. We develop the ability to experience the nature of reality as it really is – always changing. Our openness to new possibilities is anchored in a deeper internal strength that does not require us to defend the familiar. Creativity is set free in a new way and choices are more grounded. We settle into a new structure of our identity. Forgiveness and compassion for oneself and the world can arise in a new way.

But the cycle does not end here. The process continues, most likely in the form of a spiral. The fourth field is brought back to the first field by our desire to settle into the familiar and our longing for internal and external security. We build a new world of apparent stability in which we believe we have all the explanations we need. We know how the world works. We know how to lead. And the cycle begins to turn again.

Like any other model, this is an idealized aspect of reality. It reflects our constant change and the idea of a cyclical rather than linear personal development that occurs on our leadership journey. We grow organically, in non-linear ways, and, analogous to life's changes, in a continual process of disintegration on this level and re-integration on the next level. This implies that there is no end to such learning, no once-and-forever settling into a state of generative flow and deeper awareness. The pattern of our identity and our contribution to the world as a leader might slowly change over time as a result of learning, and subsequently the four fields might take on a different form, but I believe the underlying rhythm will remain essentially the same. Crises might become less ferocious and as our ability to reflect increases we might move more easily through the different fields, but we will still move and not stand still in any one of them. The way we process disintegration and re-integration sets the pattern for our learning. No two persons go through this cycle in the same way. What does become clear is that without reflection, there will be no generative stability on a higher level. And without the development of awareness and the growing capacity to reflect on our actions, no reflective instability will occur.

If reflection and awareness of the nature of reality don't truly enter the equation, it is likely that we will get stuck between non-reflective stability and non-reflective instability. We will do our personal emergency management and avoid deeper transformation. This can work for quite a long time. Our choices will be more reactive – we will seek quick solutions to seemingly superficial problems. We can become very skilled at the art of avoidance. But when we intend to reconsider our leadership contribution, we cannot run away from initiating a deeper inquiry and open ourselves to more profound change.

The charming aspect of the model is that it invites us to accept that life is about constant change. We can give up the illusion of linear growth, and the hope of final clarity in the development of our personality as a leader. Rather than asking ourselves how and when we'll reach a state of generative stability, we might humbly learn to go through each field with even-mindedness, welcoming each as we enter it. Generative stability will occur too. Evolution unfolds without force, if we do not prevent it from doing so. It is the delicate balance between our willpower and our allowing the creative unfolding to take place that determines both our journey and our leadership contribution. Responsive awareness as the ability to respond to life's feedback is an art we can develop. The balance between what we want to make happen and what wants to happen by itself is one that requires attentive listening to our own journey, to the whole, and responsiveness to the co-evolutionary journeys of other people.

CHAPTER THREE: COHERENCE

Reflections:

How do you change? What causes you to change?

How does your attraction to power work? Can you connect with the feeling that accompanies it? What do you enjoy about the power of influence? When do you feel a 'warning'?

Have you ever felt powerless, as if nothing you could do would make a difference? How did you deal with it? How did that affect your journey?

Have you had bad experiences with people in power? How did that affect your journey?

What is your pattern of reflection and non-reflection? Stability and instability?

Chapter 3: Summary

- Life is about change, some directed consciously, some responded to unconsciously, but most of it simply experienced. We arrive at a crucial point in our leadership journey when we experience change more consciously rather than being stuck in reactive patterns.
- There is a rhythm of transformation that is particular to us. Recognizing and understanding it is helpful for the process of redefining our leadership contribution.
- Resonance with something familiar in us is an important factor for change from within. When we transform as a result of resonance we essentially reconnect with our core. We are voluntarily participating in the great feedback network of life.
- Finding our unique pattern between stability and instability helps to integrate experiences into our shifting identity. Inquiry and reflection are catalysts of this process.
- Disappointment and disillusionment are unavoidable parts of our leadership journey. How we integrate (particularly) feelings of failure and powerlessness has an enormous impact on the way we learn to handle power and influence.
- The only gateway to the transcendence of the feeling of powerlessness is acceptance – not agreement. This way the most disconcerting experience can help us to access a deeper sense of life in all its possibilities, including our own and other people's humanity.
- We cannot avoid the attraction to power on our leadership journey as the feeling of being powerful nourishes our sense of self. But we can observe and listen to the warnings. Any addiction to power separates us from our journey, from our deeper intention and ultimately from the world.

CHAPTER FOUR
AWARENESS

Awareness is curative. Our process of learning results from moments of introspection, either as a consequence of crisis or because we regularly practice contemplation. The journey to redefining and deepening our leadership contribution is a pathway to a deeper connection with the world. When we reflect, we draw meaning and coherence from a stream of experience that is riddled with incoherence. Reconstructing the history of our journey is like beginning to look at it holistically. We need to let go of our habitual way of interpreting our reality and gain the distance needed to observe it without judgement. Slowly, the underlying theme emerges. Different pieces begin to fit into the overall picture. We transform our memory by looking at the past in a different way. The value and meaning we have given to events and encounters change. There is a story we begin to hear that is uniquely ours. But it is more than that. It is a story connected to a larger story unfolding, a song in a larger piece of music.

Awareness creates coherence. If our contribution to wholeness requires finding our rhythm, becoming more at home in the Universe and overcoming a fragmented sense of self, it has at its base not just experiences, but the capacity to perceive reality in a deeper way. One aspect of this is the ability to see our own story in the midst of other stories and to gain a deeper empathy for ourselves and others. When this happens, when our heart is touched by human experience, including our own, our leadership identity shifts and develops. Deeper awareness is not self-indulgent introspection for its own sake. It is a gateway to transformation when our actions in the world do not harvest our intentions. It is a movement that helps us to heal and become whole. When mindfulness grows, an appreciation of all components of experience grows. We do not disengage from the world – we are more present in the world. We become more responsive. Leading then takes place within a different sense of freedom. When we are at home in ourselves and in the world, we become more sensitive to the conditions, as well as the genuine possibilities, of a situation. Options about action are more open and less dominated by fear and by the rigid structures of memory. This kind of openness enables us to appreciate others and our own interdependency with them in a different way. Compassion grows when the attachment to a certain image of our selves vanishes. Whether we reflect individually or collectively, through reading, or contemplating, or through moments of insight, reflection cannot be prescribed. As with all patterns in the journey, we form our own pattern of growing awareness.

Paul tested, if the structures in place in his company could permit him to pursue his new concept of leadership that he had developed over time. He gradually came closer to the origin of his quest: he always wanted to help people develop as people; to foster the aspect of *being human* even in the roughest corporate environment. The company finally offered some opportunities to convey and apply this new approach in support of emerging leaders:

> I have begun to redefine what leadership means to me and what I think it means for an organization and beyond an organization. It may be that I do have something to offer that is naturally within me that I didn't even realize was there, that I didn't quite recognize as a component of strong leadership. It has to do with empathy and levelling with people, just this whole concept of building connection and some kind of relatedness with someone and being humble, exercising some degree of humility. I am not distinguishing between organizational and general life, just truly recognizing that people are human. I have developed a form of contentedness in me that I want to radiate into the world.

He noticed his increasing ability to engage with people in a deeper way. But there was also a part of him that wanted to leave the company and join like-minded people:

> If I was true to myself I would leave the company tomorrow. I would not rush into anything, just take some space and air to see what emerges. My next step would be to be a leader on my own or be a leader in conjunction with other like-minded people.

Existing structures, both external in the form of the organization, as well as his fears, held him back and kept him on a path that he now only partly accepted as his. For Paul, the themes were recurrent – confidence, courage and trust. He sensed that leaving the company would mean to walk into the unknown, into the potentially dangerous area where there was no security, no guarantee. But intuitively he knew that there was a need for time and space, for withdrawal from the world, for internal growth undisturbed by performance demands or conventional pressure – in order to mature and to give birth.

There will always be experiences that we have difficulty aligning with our image of our identity. We are likely to have periods in which we get shut in a cage of disappointment or frustration. Reflection is a way of deconstructing experience and re-building it into a new understanding. Supportive in this process of learning and integration is the awareness that the world is an undivided whole, and that our self is not, as we erroneously perceive, separate from the world. Our search for coherence can take a different turn – the insight emerges that coherence, and all the emotions attached to it, is not something to find, to reach or to achieve, but an underlying principle of the world, no matter how we perceive the world, no matter how much our thoughts divide the whole into parts. Life is coherent. The world is already whole. We can tune into it. We cannot fall out of it. We are at home in the Universe. We need to give ourselves permission to experience it. Our heart is the best guide. When we revive our leadership quest, we are guided home. Every time we encounter incoherence we can begin to see it as an invitation to see the world anew and to weave the threads of our journey into the larger story. When we begin to connect to the whole, we begin to heal and we have come to accept that the outer application of change is only a fraction of what our leadership journey is about. An essential element of healing is that we connect with the deeper truth of our life, and, as we do this, we connect with *truth* itself. What we experience inside becomes part of our leadership contribution. A door opens to profound serenity.

When Edith sold her telecommunications business, she decided to travel for as long as she needed to redefine what her leadership contribution would be and where she would contribute. The choice narrowed down to three countries: India, Chile or South Africa, and she finally settled for South Africa. Faithful to her quest, it was a country where fragmentation needed to be healed:

> The connection between healing and leading is important, there is interrelatedness. There is no other way, on any level, the personal level, human level, inner level, the macro level or the global level. If healing does not come into play we are going to continue with the world the way we have been doing it in the past. We have to heal at all levels, if we want to have a future.

Before a healing contribution can become an essential part of our leadership journey, we need to walk the road of curative awareness. There is no shortcut to this. There is no medicine we can buy and no prefabricated programme to go through. But the knowledge of how to heal is available to all of us. Insight and the transformation of memory are part of it. Encounter and connection are another part. The growing ability to forgive ourselves and others is yet another part. Humility and compassion arise where wounds are healed. Reconciliation is a deeply human experience. It makes us more whole.

In the process of integrating our experiences and transforming our structures of memory so that they can encompass a larger whole, we will inevitably come across feelings we do not like. Some of them are fears. We would be quite happy to integrate and grow without encountering them. In some phases of our journey the demons of fear occasionally sit at our doorstep, whereas in other phases they accompany us more subtly for a longer period of time. We do not welcome any of them, and doing this is hard. There is nothing constructive about fears that encroach on our hearts and occupy our minds. I am not suggesting that we embrace fears. But I believe that, again, observation is a good start to taming demons. It is important to clarify our patterns of fear so that we don't unconsciously continue to inform our leadership by an underlying vague force of fear, even though we might have consciously redefined our leadership contribution.

Whereas vision, passion and creativity are more conscious drivers of our leadership contribution, we might realize that being afraid of something is a very strong unconscious force, too. When we look back on our leadership journey, how strong was our urge to avoid feelings of failure, quickly to get over disappointments or to win the battle against feeling insignificant? There is nothing wrong with it – this is life. But in the process of dismantling and re-integrating it is good to notice these things – just that, it is not always necessary to overcome or solve them. Fears are human and they are as old as human history. They can be very helpful in the evolutionary process, but they can also be very destructive to the process. I do not believe it is worth aiming for a state in which there is no fear, even though our collectively held model of heroic leadership would probably suggest it. What I would like to invite you to do instead is simply to observe the 'when' and 'how' of your fears. If I am right that fears consciously or unconsciously inform our leadership behaviour, unearthing this silent force for ourselves is important to clarify our contribution. We cannot abolish our fears, but we can make ourselves aware of them so that we know when and how our leadership contribution is informed by them.

Diane's leadership journey in the multinational company where she works is a promising career on the surface, but a path beset with questions on the inside. One of her unanswered questions is the difference between her way of being and what she believes in and the choice of organizations she has worked in:

> I could not really align with the organizations I have worked for. I have mostly worked for organizations that were deeply misaligned with the rhythm of or the connections with people. I have sought out organizations that have been very authoritative. There is almost this need to sort of prove my mettle in the corporate world where I find probably the most self-centred people. Yet, when I think about my fears at the personal level, the first thing is loneliness, followed by insignificance, conformity, intransigence and violence. I am truly happy in connection, and I don't sit around thinking about loneliness, but when I am truly in connection and have a great time, then I notice the ending of that connection, the loneliness and the fear. To know that is actually very useful. We remain attached to the things that we need to let go of. I know the intensity of holding on to connections that are no longer viable, simply because they appear to be better than the alternative. Becoming more deeply aware of that has helped me

CHAPTER FOUR: AWARENESS

to detach. I can see my pattern of keeping connections going almost at all costs, for the sake of not actually feeling loneliness. It is maybe the deep longing for connection. I wonder if this is what people are actually searching for in business settings, when there is such a flourishing of vision, mission, goals alignment, and at the same time on the executive level so much coaching is taking place, people actually insisting on the need that they have a deep one-on-one relationship with somebody. And there is also an element of longing for deeper recognition. If you are trying to initiate change on the executive leadership level and you all try to align with this mysterious common goal, people hope that their changes will be recognized, that they are being listened to. People just need to hear from another human being that they are doing well or not. I realized that actually executives are craving for somebody to say, 'You are doing well', or 'This is what you should do more of', or 'This is what you should do less of'. It has something to do with not becoming disconnected. I can see there is almost a dance between destruction and creation or fear and creation – they are not opposites, but part of the same thing, so if you do not acknowledge what your fear is, it doesn't allow you to fully create. You create while running away from the fear and you end up creating things that do not dissolve that fear.

When we begin the search for our patterns of fear, we are likely to come across feelings of disconnection, separateness, powerlessness, non-acceptance, ignorance, insignificance, irrelevance, or loneliness. It is as if there is a deep black hole we are afraid of falling into if we don't stop ourselves. Fears are powerful. The demons can be quite ferocious. Confronting them head on is not an easy task and might only be possible in small, digestible steps. Some demons might be sleeping and we do not want to wake them up. This is entirely justified. I am not suggesting that you confront your demons. You might realize over time that, although they will never disappear entirely, they can be tamed by observation and awareness. This is important because untamed, they take up space in our mind without us really knowing. They gain unjustifiable influence over our journey. When we intend to redefine our leadership contribution, we need gradually to become aware of what our fears are and how they have been influencing our journey. Expect resistance.

Mandy's reflection on her tendency to refuse upfront leadership positions and rather be the one in the background supporting success had surfaced as a theme of avoidance throughout her journey. Yet she was hugely successful with it. In avoiding the upfront leadership model, she developed admirable skills in enabling others to participate in the creation of future realities:

> I do have a conflict about the more conventional model of leadership that I held from the time when I was five years old sitting on the top of the jungle gym, with that image ingrained in my memory. I am not able to associate very well with that, but I am not necessarily able to articulate a clear alternative model. The desire to be part of a community, to be part of creating, but also be part of servicing it, attentive to what comes through that community and being able to allow it to change, whatever direction it seeks to take – this is a much more important part of my leadership journey now. Part of my real leadership centres on community building in larger systems. When I look back at what I normally do in client systems, it is often in all sorts of ways, mostly informal, seeking to find ways of creating communities, creating connections that don't seem obvious, enabling people to come together and have a collective voice without threatening the

structures that exist. I support people in coming together where there is a deeper desire for something that has a collective purpose. I am trying to enable that to survive, even in highly hierarchical conventional systems where that could be quite threatening or alien and unhelpful. And I realize I am doing exactly that in the work I am doing in the multinational European bank right now. It is seeking to find and enable what I can see already exists, a connected set of people who have a very common way of looking at the business. I am trying to help them come together in a way that allows them to share their thinking and to look at ways they could serve the organization or society in a different way. And that is what I do. But when somebody asks me what I do, I don't talk about that and I think that is interesting. That brings me to the question, 'What are you most afraid of?' I can see that I am afraid of being accountable and of taking a stand. When I look at my fears on the personal level, it is all about being alone and being apart. I am afraid of being the expert rather than a fellow traveller. I am afraid of standing clearly in myself and being apart from others. When I know I am in service to others, I never feel alone, because I am not alone. Because how can you serve others and be alone? But I have come to realize as good as my work is in its results, when I avoid taking the lead and being accountable, I also withhold what I believe in. I withhold parts of myself. This is fragmenting and I end up being alone. So the very thing I fear is the very thing I realize.

The purpose of unearthing your patterns of fear is that it enables freedom. Rather than being locked into your unconscious structures, you gain the very distance that finally enables you to make choices and take a different road, little by little. There is no jumpstart. But with increasing awareness you can at least begin to smile at the repetitiveness of your patterns. Do not force yourself to change. There is nothing to get rid of. Mandy's example shows that her very patterns created her strength. There is no need to eliminate them. Sometimes our unconscious reactions to fear can achieve great things. The purpose of beginning to observe the patterns is to open a door so that you can integrate what you tend to avoid, into the larger structure of your identity. With some demons tamed, you can stop splitting parts of yourself off and open up to *who* you are. With other demons tamed, you can stop blocking yourself from being *what* you are. Unconsciously lived fears keep us from becoming whole. Conscious fears are friendly companions who remind us about the need to be true to ourselves. There is an interesting connection. What we perceive as a personal fear is often connected with what we fear on a larger scale, be it in professional life or for humanity. I am aware of the role of childhood experiences in causing fears in a person's life, but the recurrence of certain fears in the conversation with leaders from very diverse backgrounds, age groups, cultural exposure and professional positions has led me to think that fears express more than an entirely personal issue. They come across almost as the expression of a deeper wound that seems to be so universal that it cannot only be the result of one person's childhood experience. To unearth these fears, to accept them beyond the acknowledgement of one's personal history, could possibly open ourselves to a deeper level of compassion. There is a common thread of human experience discernable in the fears people express, no matter in which cultural context they were born, how old they are or which positions they hold.

The acknowledgement of the universal character of our fears is helpful when we begin to see that these are not just our fears, but deeply human fears. These fears are holding up a mirror for us to become aware of what we feel needs to be changed and healed in

CHAPTER FOUR: AWARENESS

the world. The need for healing that we have picked up on as our very personal fear is often what we unconsciously or very actively try to heal in the world and so informs our leadership journey. By pursuing the healing of the world, we hope to be healed as well.

A process of healing requires the kind of reflection that widens our perspective, lets us see connections, and makes us conscious of being part of a larger whole. It is meant to shift the focus of our attention. If reflection does not take place and life's feedback is not acknowledged, no integration of experiences can take place, and the understanding of the relationship between our identity and that of others and the world remains fragmented. The potential for a gradual reorganization or deepening of our identity is lost. Awareness, then, is one step on the road to deeper humility, compassion and more clarity of mind. This is rarely a spectacular event on our journey, but a slow process of accepting the forces of life, reviving our energy to contribute and taking reality exactly as it is. Reflection releases mind space that has been hidden by habitual patterns of reaction and memory. We unlock our behavioral patterns.

But there is much more to the role of awareness as an essential element of the redefinition of your leadership journey. Awareness is one step toward the cultivation of our mind. If we take this road seriously, we are invited into a deeper understanding of the relationship between mind and matter, of thought and manifest reality. Both collectively and individually, thought creates reality beyond the immediately obvious. If our mind in its particular configuration has an impact beyond what we would commonly believe, then there is a certain responsibility for us, particularly when we lead, to be alert to the movement of thought. Without such awareness we might simply extend our own patterns of thought into the world, whether beneficial or harmful, healthy or pathological. Unawareness and a lack of understanding about the role of thought and consciousness can potentially cause harm. Gradually, deepening insight into the intrinsic relationship between mind and matter prevents us from falling prey to the common assumption that reality as we experience it is a given fact, a world outside ourselves that we need to react to, cope with, conquer, or influence. Acknowledging that there might be a link between thought and manifest reality helps us to see its impact, individually and collectively, in bringing forth the world as we envision it. There is a promise – this could help us to lead more consciously for the benefit of the future.

A Glimpse into Theory: The Cognitive Perspective on Mind and Ethics

In his lectures on ethical know-how which he held in Italy in 1991, Francesco Varela notes that cognitive science slowly awakens to the idea of perception as something entirely different from the recognition or representation of a pre-given external world (Bateson, 2000; Capra, 1996). For Francesco Varela, it is self-evident that cognition can only be understood properly as 'embodied', and that the world we know is not pre-given, but enacted through the history of our processes of cognition in a constant cycle between perception and creation. Mind, for him, is a movement, not a static element. Our cognitive structures emerge from our perception and actions in the world, and vice versa (Varela, 1999). The key feature of perception is a highly cooperative network, not a linear abstraction of information. In neurophysiological terms information processing is a 'multidirectional multiplicity' (p. 48) where 'signals move 'back and forth' gradually becoming more coherent until a microworld has been constituted' (Varela, 1999, p. 48 and 49). When we look at it from this scientific point of view, there is no central agent thinking, there is no thinker behind thought. In Buddhist insights there is no knower behind the known (Macy, 1991). Both modern cognitive science and Buddhist thought come to the conclusion that there is no identifiable or localized self. We behave, think, act, and cognize as a functioning unit without any 'I' being present. The 'I' is constructed by its own faculty of cognizing, but it has no substance, no reality other than the convenient agreement for language proposes. This is a shocking, almost absurd idea. If there is no 'I', who is reading this? The narrative we tell about our *virtual self* is so strong and we are so entrenched in having built this particular virtual entity, that seeing through it into the plane of reality behind the construction, is a difficult step. It is almost a dangerous step – we must perceive it as threatening, or irritating at the very least. The reason that Francesco Varela pursues the idea of the virtuality of our self so relentlessly is that he assumes that there is a close connection between a deeper understanding of the self as virtual and the arising of *ethical know-how*. The hypothesis is this – if we begin to cultivate our mind through practices of contemplation and meditation, we can enter into the plane of reality that lies beyond the construction of our self. When we do so, we not only begin to experience a more profound freedom, we also access our 'ethical know-how' (as Francesco Varela calls it) in a more profound way. To put it more simply – the less we keep our mind busy with the construction and reconstruction of our 'I' (fears play an important part in this), the more space opens in our mind for natural compassion towards all that is. Ethical behaviour is a natural consequence of it. When we see beyond the construction of our identity, the concern for the larger whole of which we are all part becomes second nature.

This is not about acquiring skills to become a different and better personality, adopting moral values conceptually and developing into an enhanced being. Rather, it is the removal of habitual and historical blocks that keep us from perceiving the true nature of reality. Drawing on the teachings of the Confucian Meng-tzu who lived around the fourth century BC, Francesco Varela reminds us of the Eastern view of human nature as naturally good and capable of being ethical. In this view, awareness and the cultivation of the mind lead us to become naturally responsive to the needs of others. Though this is gained through courage, persistence, practice and patience, in its essence this is no more than activating our natural disposition. 'It is as if one were born already knowing how to play the violin and had to practice with great exertion in order to remove the habits that prevented one from displaying that virtuosity' (ibid. p. 72). The cultivation of this inner disposition is a journey of constant experience and learning. The natural state of the mind is one of compassion and experiential awareness of the emptiness of the self. Francesco Varela admits that it is very alien to Western thought that the faculty of caring and compassion does not only reside at the ground of human beings, but can be developed through the sustained practice of cultivating the mind. But he believes that the idea is worth entertaining as he proposes that the application and understanding of ethical behaviour needs to take place in a non-moralistic framework. He humbly suggests that what the world needs is contemplative disciplines that support letting go of the ego and help uncover the compassion human beings are capable of. Mere rational and intellectual thought would not be able to achieve the same (ibid. p. 73). Francesco Varela adds an interesting thought – he cautions us to not confuse the readily available Western schemes for personal self-improvement with such a profound contemplative discipline. In his view, the achievement orientation of Western culture is almost entirely based on the cultivation of a sense of self and increases rather than reduces its illusionary importance. The result would be the opposite of what is intended by a practice of cultivation of the mind.

Awareness begins with observation and reflection. In whatever way we integrate reflection into our leadership journey, it helps us to slowly cut through the chains of habitual thought patterns or preconceptions and their subsequent actions. But there is a trap waiting for us. If our mind is conditioned by a model of leadership that requires the continuous acquisition of skills, we might confuse reflection with perfection. Seeing the need for internal development as a process of perfecting our leadership abilities is not wrong, but it is only part of the story. Although the focus on self-development and personal mastery is important for a pragmatic approach to our leadership endeavour, it can lead to a conceptual trap with enormous impact. The perception of an expanding, ever-growing, to-be-fulfilled self, and a more and more stable and continuous identity, could create blindness towards the interdependence of our being with all that we are not. It reinforces our illusion of a fragmented world, in which we ourselves are yet another agent battling to become fulfilled. The attention on 'self' development can make us attached to a certain image of our personality. We might imagine a radiant and influential leadership identity for ourselves, and as we walk this road we become victims of our own illusion and ignorance. There is a dilemma: self-awareness and self-observation are of utmost importance when we want to understand our leadership journey and redefine our contribution. Without growing awareness about ourselves, our interaction in the world, our choices would remain blind and unconsciously informed by previous choices and the way our cognition habitually selects. Reflective awareness is a prerequisite for growing into our true potential. Yet when we fall foul of wanting to perfect our identity, we begin to walk on the opposite path – away from our true potential, away from the world. Awareness is about expanding our understanding about us and the world, not about acquiring skills or creating an image of our leadership identity. The more aware we become, and the more we integrate experience, the less important we become. Awareness is our road to humility. We need to understand ourselves in order to understand the world. Seeing the world 'as it is', is an ever-expanding process requiring a commitment to truth and a willingness to discover the unknown. *Rather than becoming more perfect, we become more human.* Perception of reality as it is becomes the perception of multiple realities as we see ourselves in context and gain a profound empathy with the human experience. Curiosity grows. Certainty diminishes. We travel the journey from the heart. As we become more human we can see our uniqueness and our gifts, yet we also see ourselves as being part of a collective evolution. It helps to accept the interconnected nature of reality. Our leadership journey is only partly a process of acquiring knowledge, skills and competencies. To a large extent it is a gradual process of deepening our understanding of reality and feeling at home in a participatory universe. It is helpful to begin to conceive of our self and our identity not as fixed entities but as processes in constant development as a result of continually integrating experience.

We become open to more possibilities – other than those in our current view of reality. The freedom of choice grows.

Diane has been very active in supporting women in her company and has recently managed to organize dialogue circles for women in management. These circles open up the possibility for them to see both their own and their collective development in a different

CHAPTER FOUR: AWARENESS

way. This is important for her as she believes that individual and collective awareness can have a profound impact on changing the way leadership models are handled in her company:

> The less aware one is the more automatic and habitual, and ultimately the more maintaining, one is regarding one's identity. The more aware one is the more one is able to get to the heart of what one is and therefore one can truly choose to maintain or develop. Then there is a constant tension between wanting to be familiar and comfortable, and confident with who one is and allowing the push into the unknown, and then seeing what happens. To my mind, awareness is almost like slowing down a moving picture to the point that everything is in slow motion. It is the kind of awareness that is required to look at whirlpools in a river and draw them.

Awareness is like a handbrake we can pull up in the speed of events. As long as we are either not used to doing this or we ignore its benefits as we rush through the days, we are caught in a cycle of action and reaction that leaves us little space for choices that are informed by a deeper understanding of ourselves or our path. We often perceive others to be the cause of our discomfort and negative reactions. We battle to keep up with life's events and often feel like victims tossed around in a storm that is not of our own making. We feel alone and separate, battling to maintain our identity in an increasingly demanding world. When we have subjected ourselves to this way of seeing the world, reflection reaches us in its cruder forms: through crises, disease, obstacles. This, at least, forces us to step back. From then on, we might learn to include regular observation and contemplation in our everyday life. Getting into the habit of quick reflections and brief evaluations of the course we're taking is the first step on the road to awareness. But

CHAPTER FOUR: AWARENESS

I suggest doing more than that – in reconstructing the history of your journey and tracking all the different streams like your early intention, your quest, your patterns of reflection, your fears, your relationship with feedback and change, you are led into a world of coherence. When you identify the patterns of your behaviour, of events, experiences, feelings and achievements, you also discover the way your mind constructs reality. You begin to access the deeper storyline – your aspirations, dreams, intentions and what matters to your heart. You access your genuine love of life, with which, I am sure, all of us were born. When you begin to understand how your leadership identity has formed, you pass through a gateway. You begin to drop the idea that it is all about you. You might smile at your latent hope for grandeur and your silent tendency to dream of omnipotence. You can reconcile with the resilient narcissism of your self. It will probably dawn on you how long the road to real mindfulness is. But you also awaken to the possibility of taking a road that is greatly facilitated by meditation. As you integrate a larger range of possibilities into your life, you can look at human experience from different angles with suspended judgement. There is a strange equation here – as you become more whole your self becomes less important. As you develop inner serenity you become more concerned with others, with the world. Sometimes the result is a total shift in consciousness, and the deep desire to serve takes root.

This is not part of Diane's official job description, but in tracking her leadership history she notices that she has always been interested in serving people whose voices are weak, or those who have no voice:

> I feel accountable to people or groups who don't have a voice, who are not being heard. If I see myself taking a leadership role then that's who I am serving more consciously now. It

CHAPTER FOUR: AWARENESS

has been there all along, but now in the middle of my career I want to put this intent into action more constructively. In my own sphere, I have begun to mentor younger women. This is not a burden, I enjoy doing it. I am finding ways out of some of my habitual patterns of disconnection and begin to connect emerging young women who may not have enough contacts. Sometimes I am just there so that they have somebody to talk to. I have also come to realize that that is what I enjoy – whether it is being appreciated by the company or not, is not so important anymore, rather it is important that it is appreciated by the person I can help.

The way the process of growing awareness takes place cannot be predicted. We form our pattern of growing awareness differently from anybody else. This is not about becoming more successful as a leader; it is about becoming more true to yourself. If success follows, it originates in the depth of your intention. Entering in the field of mind, even through a small window, sensing the vast dimensions of reality, reaches into our hearts. Truth, not the intellectually correct standpoint, but the intuitive knowing about reality resonates on a deeper emotional level. When we glimpse the larger story that our story is woven into, we are drawn to participate in helping this larger story to unfold. A commitment to lead that stems from having seen through a window into the nature of reality is a different kind of commitment because we're committing to the underlying potential of evolution. Once we have arrived there, we begin to see that absence of awareness does not help the world. We also notice that it does not bring forth the world in a meaningful way when we shy away from bringing out our creative potential. False modesty is not humility. We are here to unfold and, with our unfoldment, to contribute to the course the world takes. It *does* matter how we are, what we think, or what we do. A deeper understanding of ourselves leads us to let go of the preoccupation with our own importance. We can stop futilely fighting to live a fulfilled life. It is all here.

Humility sometimes arrives with the realization that the world is larger by far than our perception can reach, that our contribution to sustain life counts, and it is essential and possible to serve. Contribution will no longer spring from the desire to excel or get it right, nor from the hope of leaving a legacy, but from the insight that the deepest nature of humanness is to contribute to evolution constructively. The cultivation of the mind is thus not a selfish exercise with a narcissistic, repetitive focus on the self, but a road to connecting the individual mind with the vast sea of consciousness. Perceiving and eventually experiencing consciousness as one and the world as a whole, even though it might feel like a theoretical proposition in the beginning, changes our thinking processes at the core. Our thought patterns are reassembled and we see the world and ourselves from a different perspective. Since we co-create the world to a large extent through our thinking processes, this could well contribute to making a constructive difference in the world, however minor. Then again, if our leadership action is accompanied by an inner process of growing awareness, it might contribute to real transformation.

The generative process of life is a continuous dance of creation, conservation and passing away. We are part of this cycle. Through our internal world of balance and imbalance we co-create the external world. There is always the possibility for new life. We have a timeless connection with life's renewal. Our continuous participation in the flow of generation, degeneration and regeneration is a dance we can neither stop nor leave. We can only take part in it in a more conscious and life-sustaining way.

Sustainable generation requires a combination of different energies in order to unfold enfolded energy into existence, maintain its

CHAPTER FOUR: AWARENESS

growth and enable life-sustaining patterns to manifest. These energetic principles can be found in our intentions, and interactions and actions in the world, individually and collectively. When they are in balance or in a healthy rhythm life is brought forth in a sustainable way. If the rhythm is erratic, the pattern gets out of balance. Translated into the realm of leadership, I believe what we need is a balanced rhythm of passion, contemplation and commitment (see page 247). It is worthwhile looking at the way we balance these energies on our leadership journey.

When I describe passion as an arousal of the heart, it is the desire to make a difference, the urge to change something for the better. *Passion is at the base of creativity and inspiration.* When we feel passionate, we know why we are here and why we're doing what we're doing, and we can inspire others. Our initial deeper intention is nourished by passion. Dreams hold passion, as do aspirations. Passion is the direct expression of our capacity to love life, the world and other people. Sometimes, over long periods of time on our leadership journey, passion lives a remote life in our heart. We hardly remember the feeling. When passion is missing, our contribution lacks strength and spirit, the difference we want to make fades. Our contribution is likely manifesting far below its potential. Our attraction to the deeper force of life is faint. Our joy in actively participating in the dance is at a low ebb. We become disconnected from our heart. We begin to settle for the substitute – we let ourselves be driven by superficial stimulation and the desire to excel. We take on more and more new challenges, frequently change jobs, engage in extreme sports or indulge in stimulants. We become restless in our unconscious search to access the deeper force of life that is the source of genuine passion. We focus on outward achievement only. With unbalanced stimulation we are likely to move rapidly towards burn-out. This is all human. But I believe it is worth observing. There might be the danger that the habit of mistaking the substitute for the real thing is taking us away from giving the world our real gifts. If we cannot answer the question of what we are passionate about on our leadership journey, it is worth pulling up the handbrake and beginning a search. We need to renew our quest. There is a journey waiting for us.

Without commitment and perseverance, life cannot be maintained. We need the confidence that things will work out if we hold to the energy strongly enough. The generative process depends on this caring and nourishing in order to flourish. When this is missing our leadership intention cannot really grow, it cannot be sustained. We know this – patterns of self-sabotage through lack of patience, our fear of repetitiveness and boredom becoming so overwhelming that we make frequent restarts without ever achieving what we set out to, settling for less then we expected because we stop believing that things will work out. Or we subtly fall prey to the opposite – we get caught in obligations that we have built around us like a cage, we do not want to change the way we do things or we have created a net of security around us that is holding our creativity at bay. We experience periods of self-denial and over-commitment at the expense of our health and creativity.

A strong and balanced energy of commitment in leadership can take the form of determination accompanied by a deeper knowing that what we hold deep in our heart will manifest. Commitment is also expressed through our caring patience and the constant and reliable nourishing of what we have decided to take responsibility for. We can endure difficulties, and overcome obstacles.

Without contemplation, we are victims of our own actions. Times of inner and outer silence, collectively and individually, are a way of processing the realities emerging from passion and commitment. Reflective energy is regenerative and transformative. Insights gain the space and time to surface. The qualities are those of stillness and waiting, of sinking into a deeper level of existence that builds and dismantles constantly without our interference. The energy of contemplation holds the capacity simply to observe what is happening and become conscious of our patterns of action in life's processes. Sustainable generative processes need renewal in silence, patiently waiting things into existence. They need trust and 'not-acting', they need to be allowed time to mature. When this is missing, our contribution becomes unstable, as if it lacked the kind of confidence and trust an innocent child has. When our intention to create has too much force and too little space to grow by itself, it lacks strength and withers. If we do not become conscious of this danger, we might reactively fall into the opposite state – we want to withdraw from the world, disengage and disconnect, we become depressed. Our contribution seems to be irrelevant and insignificant.

Lucia is in the process of discovering her leadership potential. Despite her ambivalence to the culture of power and her careful observation of leaders, she enjoys the dynamic speed of her corporate environment and the possibilities that open up for her. She has held different positions in the company in a relatively short period, has been recommended for the fast track to leadership development, and is about to move into a new position in the headquarters of the multinational company she works for:

> I never thought about passion, having passion for something I do that would not only let me do the necessary in the short term, but carry me through the obstacles and the delays. I actually thought, 'I enjoy my job, but I do not have passion for it'. I do think when you are in an organization with a lot of internal politics this is what kills passion. It is not so difficult to find something that you have passion for, but more difficult having the space to follow through on something and do what you believe is right. This is my fifth job in three and a half years, which is a lot, and I'm beginning to think it is

good to ask questions. I now have a position where there is space for contemplation; the success of my job depends on it and on the quality of my engagement. I can see a much bigger picture, things are getting clearer, things I have known and been aware of, suddenly click into place and I immediately understand the implications on the bigger picture. If I neglected anything in the past, it is probably contemplation – it was entirely covered by stimulation and commitment to the job because I was put in an operational role where this was important. In a way, I can see that I do have an issue around commitment, somehow I have neglected that. It would require sustained passion, and sometimes your passion can be affected when you are having a bad day, a bad conversation, or somebody makes you feel bad or you feel the impact of politics and rigid organizational structures. For me, I notice that as soon as my passion starts going my commitment starts going. I am attracted to the vision of something. I do not like the unglamorous side of commitment, which is attention to something over a long time. I know I have a tendency to avoid the implementation, the execution and the details. I can see how much the space for contemplation is needed to get this balanced. I think that is also where all this executive education comes from; it is not just to educate people, but to make space for contemplation. I can see it with my former boss. His coach was his oxygen. He needed the time to sit back and reflect. When you take away the opportunity for contemplation you are not realizing the best in people.

The first step is always observation. What is your natural rhythm? What is your focus, what do you tend to neglect? What is the sequence of events that you can track to identify the pattern? What do you prefer to avoid? What do you avoid unconsciously? The reality is that our lives tend to be unbalanced. But I believe there is a deeper force in us that pulls us back into balance – not that we always understand the message. But if we observe more closely how this rhythm works and what the effects are of it being more or less in balance, we become more attentive to serious imbalances. We can be more active in rebalancing our generative rhythm.

John holds a management position in organizational change in a multinational company in the United States. His leadership is deeply informed by his religious upbringing. When he was younger he wanted to be a leader in the church, because he saw this as being at the forefront of changing the world. In his early twenties he had great aspirations to help make the world a better place. His strength was in bringing people together, making connections across groups, and helping people to be the best they could be. He did extremely well at school, college and university and his family expected him to have a brilliant career based on thoroughly religious values. Early on his leadership journey he encountered a period of severe exhaustion:

> I had a genuine mid-life crisis at the age of 29. I didn't know who I was, what I wanted to do with my life, and whether the religion I had been raised in all my life was true or valid for me and my journey. I began to question things I had never questioned before, particularly my assumptions about the way the world works and my role in it. I had assumed that everything was black and white, right or wrong, with no middle ground between the two. I felt I needed to be a responsible person – all of a sudden I wanted nothing to do with responsibility. I changed my thesis to focus on personal change, and I didn't do anything that didn't help me in one way or another. I even considered leaving school and taking my wife and two children to live in the desert. I ended up taking a 10-month sabbatical to learn about different things and

> experience the world as a non-responsible adult. I completed every personality assessment I could find and turned inward and towards creating inner peace with my journey in life.

His time off formed his identity and opened him up to questions he would not have asked otherwise:

> I realized that a true leader does not seek to become a leader. Instead, they do the work that they have passion for and then others are attracted to what they are doing. They become leaders not by design, but as a result. Up until that point, I had consciously strived to become a leader. This had a tremendous impact on me, for it undid all my assumptions about my leadership journey in my life. It begged all kinds of questions for me: What did I believe in for myself and not simply because I thought I should believe in this? What are my values? What is my passion?

John tried out various paths with successes and failures and finally joined the multinational corporation. This allowed him to reconnect with both his tremendous skills and his early aspirations:

> It has been the most difficult five years of my life professionally, but also the most rewarding and full of growth. Something has happened here that I have not had in other organizations. It has helped me to create connections and bonds that have not otherwise been possible for me.

Crises do not always have an easily understandable purpose. Not every crisis leads to deeper reflection or a reconnection with our deeper intention and our deeply held values. But they are a form of rebalancing and it is worthwhile to discover the underlying positive natural intent in them. The outcome of learning is unpredictable. The more fear and anxiety are unconsciously part of our journey, the less are we able to find meaning in the turning points. We keep ourselves busy with weathering the storm and tackling the fear. We search frantically for our purpose, which will not reveal itself by force. We only begin to relax when we see the pattern beneath the surface of reality. When we begin to let go of our ambitions for our leadership image, we can move into a different space. Everything becomes possible, failure and success, recognition and rejection, happiness and depression. It is all part of the whole that we are. When we return to our heart's quest, we can reconcile with the diversity of experience. Our growing resilience to the storms of life is based on an inner balance that does not reject experience, but knows its changeable nature. We can unfold meaning from the most difficult circumstances. We can feel at home.

Lesley got a degree in law because she had always loved helping people find a voice:

> There was something about advocating for others as a theme: When I wanted to be a lawyer, that is what I wanted to do, the whole idea of getting out there to battle on the legal front. I was really quite attracted to the idea of going to court and making really quite decisive speeches and posing very tricky questions, deciding right from wrong. There is a huge element of that inside me, even now. I think that is a big theme that I need to refine. That is something I have passion for, it gets me going every time I think something is wrong, helping people find a voice when they don't have one.

Lesley is now in her late thirties and has held a number of management positions in human resources in two different multinational companies and a large bank in the United Kingdom. When she left the bank it was because of a profound lack of meaning. She could not connect anymore with the work she was asked to do. Her leadership weakened until her team confronted her and she heard herself speaking openly from the heart, explaining to them that the values lived within the bank were so intensely misaligned with her own that she would probably have to leave: 'I got to the stage where I was utterly exhausted. I just did not fit in with the values and course of the organization and it was becoming harder and harder for me to perform.' As she was getting more and more disconnected from the organization's intention, she was also losing her voice in her professional position and failed to live up to her colleagues' expectations. The disconnection weakened her strong leadership capacity, which had always been a feature of her journey. Separated from her deeper intention and her heart's desire, passion went missing and she could not sustain the commitment her leadership position required. Neither could she find her real voice, as the pressure of the situation built up. She decided to leave the bank. She did not fill the sudden emptiness quickly but allowed time for contemplation and experimentation with work affiliations that were closer to her heart:

> I am at a sort of resting point, coming off the motorway. I was stuck on the motorway and I was going really, really fast and probably not in the right direction. I think I have the capacity to make a huge amount of difference, somewhere, somehow, to some people. I don't know what that is, but if I could gather the experience I have and my personality traits, my characteristics, and really harness that behind something, it could be hugely powerful. But I don't know what that thing is right now.

How our generative rhythm takes place between passion, commitment and contemplation is probably not only a result of our own inner pattern, but is strongly influenced by values and demands from outside, particularly organizational cultures and leadership fashions. Performance appraisals value only certain parts of us and least of all our ability to reflect. In adapting to the dynamics and energy flow in the organization we work in, we might begin to neglect the healthy flow of our own energies. The reciprocity between our individual journey and the leadership requirements of the corporate world mount up to a complex interdependence of blocks and flow. It is important to notice misalignments, even when we cannot draw immediate conclusions from them. If we ignore the natural tendency of rebalancing, we unconsciously create outside forces to shift our pattern of energies. More particularly, when we are stuck in a cycle of stimulation and passionless commitment, something external will push us into contemplation. There is no other way out. The inert tendency to reinstate the flow is a key feature of life.

There is a symptom of imbalance over time that we all know – disorientation. We do not know what our path is. There is vagueness about how we want to participate in life and leading. We do what we do, but we would not be able to explain it to anybody else. This is also part of the journey; periods of clarity are followed by periods of vagueness, and vice versa. But when we help our rhythm to flow more freely there are more opportunities to reconnect with the essence of our journey. We progressively gain more clarity. We integrate more easily and are less likely to be tossed about in the storms of life. There is an extraordinary phenomenon. When we begin to find our unique rhythm, our balance of the generative process, we begin to connect more deeply with life's creativity. As a result the way we think about our leadership contribution changes. Passion is likely to develop into compassion, a more profound attention to the world's needs rather than our own fulfillment. We feel called to participate in different undertakings. We begin to know that our gifts count. It is worthwhile not only developing them but bringing them into the world. We sense that our deepest intention, however naïve it may have been at the time, is valuable enough to make it worth living more actively. When we have passed through the needle's eye of self-acceptance, our commitment changes – rather than seeing it as a mixture between willpower and obligation, we feel it developing into an attitude of self-less service. We are here to serve the world and to bring forth evolution. Our intention matures. When we acknowledge the need for stillness and are less afraid of encountering the void, we notice that our phases of contemplation contribute to a slowly developing even-mindedness. We can see the whole. This is when our generative energy matures. What was once vague becomes clearer. We begin to gain easier access to what we feel needs doing in the world.

When the energies flow freely and in balance, what we are capable of bringing into this world shows up more clearly. We might suddenly remember an unrealistic dream and discover that it's possible now. Or we give attention to an idea that has accompanied us for a while but we never had the time to pursue. Or we have an intention that was at the bottom of our heart more openly. Or we suddenly notice that we have known all along that we need to do something different and now have the courage to do it. Or we discover that we can do what we always did, but in a different, more meaningful way.

This is rarely a process of sudden revelations. It is a process of slowly growing into your true potential. With the energies balancing more and more, our generative centre unfolds and becomes a more conscious part of our leadership journey. There is no sudden breakthrough, no purpose to reveal in an instant. Expect to enjoy the journey rather than get attached to your expectation of a meaningful life. The work continues. Your mind is the keeper of your identity as much as the gatekeeper to compassion and perception of the larger whole. In the process of deepening your awareness, you cannot prevent your mind from redefining your leadership contribution. As you move into deeper layers of consciousness, your preoccupation with yourself withers. You begin to listen from the whole. There is a wonderful story told by the violinist Miha Pogacnik and captured by Otto Scharmer from a personal conversation:

> When I gave my first concert in Chartres I felt that the cathedral almost kicked me out. For I was young and I tried to perform as I always did: just playing my violin. But then I came to realize that in Chartres you actually cannot play your small violin, but you have to play the macro violin. The small violin is the instrument that is in your hands. The macro violin is the whole cathedral that surrounds you. The cathedral of Chartres is entirely built according to musical principles. Playing the macro violin requires you to listen and to play from another place. You have to move your listening and playing from within to beyond yourself. (Pogacnik, personal conversation, quoted in Scharmer, 2000, p. 13)

CHAPTER FOUR: AWARENESS

Reflections:

What are you most afraid of in your personal life?

What are you most afraid of in your professional life?

What are you most afraid of on a global scale?

How does this relate to your leadership journey?

What is your relationship with the energies of passion, commitment and contemplation? What patterns can you identify? What do you tend to neglect? What to you tend to focus on? Which rhythm can you identify?

What do you think is at the centre of the three energies?

If you were absolutely true to yourself, what would be the next steps on your leadership journey?

Chapter 4: Summary

- Awareness is curative. Our process of learning occurs as a result of moments of inward-looking, be they as a consequence of crises or a result of contemplation.
- An important aspect on the road to awareness is the ability to see our own story in the midst of other stories and thereby gain deeper empathy for ourselves and others.
- Awareness is not self-indulging introspection. It is a gateway to personal transformation that helps us match our actions in the world with our deeper intentions.
- We are at home in the Universe. When we revive our leadership quest we are guided home, and as we become more whole, our self becomes less important. With more inner serenity we begin to feel the desire to serve the world more strongly.
- It helps us tremendously to acknowledge the demons of our fears, which may at times sit at our doorstep. Unearthing the patterns of our fears is important in understanding the way in which they have informed our leadership journey.
- Humility often arrives as the realization that although the world is far larger than we can comprehend, our contribution counts and it is possible genuinely to serve.
- The generative process of life and leading is a dance of creation, conservation and passing away. In this dance the energies of passion, commitment and contemplation (or rest) sustain life. It is worthwhile looking at how we balance these energies on our leadership journey.

CHAPTER FIVE
CONTRIBUTION

I believe that listening from beyond ourselves is not something we can learn to do. It is a natural result of increasing mindfulness or a sudden insight into the nature of reality. However, we can prevent ourselves from feeling the nature of the cathedral. We can watch in awe without noticing that that nature is not something outside ourselves, it is something we are part of. We can also remove the obstacles that lie between us and our capacity to perceive the larger whole that we are part of, as it unfolds. Awareness about our leadership journey is like clearing the path towards awareness of the whole. On the way to playing the macro-violin in the cathedral of Chartres there are many small steps to understanding ourselves better and subsequently understanding reality. In the meantime we become less occupied with the maintenance of all the pressing images of our identity, and at the same time we notice that what we do and do not do, what we think and do not think, is much more important than we imagined. It has an impact. We participate in the unfolding of evolution whatever we choose to contribute or withhold. We know that, to a great extent, it is our choice to live our life and our leadership the way we do. But we also realize that as individuals we can change the world, no matter how small that change might be. We can make a difference. But how do we know what counts?

A couple of years ago I had a visitor staying in my home. He was a businessman from India who for most of his career was very successfully involved in the construction industry in India. He was an engineer by training and had been managing several building companies in major Indian cities. In the second half of his career, he consciously decided to change his business model – he handed over all his companies to his son, sold other parts and also sold most

CHAPTER FIVE: CONTRIBUTION

of his real estate. He kept what he needed to keep the family going and pursued one of his earlier dreams – to create farms on which plants for natural diversity and plants for agricultural production would be mixed in a way that benefited both the commercial harvest and the people who lived and worked on the farm. He had a little cottage on one of his farms where he could spend time meditating. His farm workers knew that the profits they generated were saved for the purchase of new farms and, to a larger extent, were donated to meditation centres. He himself meditated and taught in his tradition in India and other parts of the world. When he sat in my living room he explained to me:

> The first half of your life you spend exploring the world and yourself. You take in and take in; the world serves your own growth. The second half of your life you spend giving back and you do this for the rest of your life. You serve the world and you serve people. It is important not to miss that turning point. So what is your contribution? What do you serve?

I did not have an instant answer to his question and it took a few moments before I realized that he did not expect one. When we begin to sense that our leadership contribution needs to be reconsidered, a question like this strikes us like a sudden uncomfortable memory. We are pushed beyond our comfort zone. We have enough demands placed on us; we do not need more. Our first emotional reaction is to defend what we do and why we do not do anything else. Our second reaction is to find a more rational explanation of how we actually do serve. We find ways of justifying our engagement in the world the way it is. We tell ourselves all the little ways in which we actually do serve the world. Our third reaction is to doubt ourselves. What difference can we make anyway other than what we do already, probably even trying hard to satisfy our own and others' needs and live up to our own and others' expectations? Who are we to make a difference? Our fourth reaction is to doubt the question. Why would it make a difference, if we served the world? It is fine for some people but we do not need to be among them. Not everybody needs to be altruistic. This might apply to some but not to all. The world is not an ideal place and we have to accept this as a fact. So why us?

The question remained in my mind for years. As with all questions that aim directly at the heart, it became a constant reminder of my journey. It took a year or two before I was finally prepared to grow slowly into an answer. If we allow that to happen, such questions reach our heart. We know when we set out on our journey that this is what we intuitively wanted to do – serve the world. We might have become far more realistic, much more sensible, and slightly more cynical. But we sense the underlying quest. The purpose of our early intention was to do something for the benefit of humankind. The history of our journey shows that we were concerned. There had been times when we believed we could make a difference. We needed to grow and mature; we discovered the world and tested ourselves. Life took us to many internal and external places. But now, the time has come to say *Yes* to the commitment of living in answer to that question – *what is my contribution to a more sustainable world?* The underlying search for meaning will lead us back to our quest. We hold essentially human values. There is a thread throughout our leadership journey that is never completely lost. When we develop our capacity to transcend experiences and make sense of them, we do increase our ability to listen to the cathedral's sound. Making sense of experience does not require finding out what caused what and why something happened; there is no need to look for a hidden plan or a predictive path, because there is none. I do *not* believe in a singular purpose, our purpose. There is nothing pre-designed. Nobody has taken charge other than we ourselves.

CHAPTER FIVE: CONTRIBUTION

In as much as our leadership journey is unique, it could also have taken a different direction if there had been a different combination of choice and encounter. We do have unique gifts, but how we apply them is not laid out before us. The range of possibilities is manifold, undetermined and endless.

It makes no sense to wait for a call. We might never hear it. When we see other people seemingly following a call, it should not bother us. Our path might be different. We have choices, and we can reconsider our contribution every day. We do not need a sudden awakening, a once-and-for-all clarity. For many of us, redefining our leadership contribution is a road to freedom travelled slowly. In the beginning, there is vagueness because we don't know how things will be different from the way they are today. There is hesitation because we have built a life that we do not want to dismantle. We probably do not need to. We can take one step at a time. There is no need for radical change. We can slowly grow into a more profound leadership contribution. Once our heart is committed and our intention is revived, we will find the means for our own maturation.

I have invited you to track the history of your leadership journey because it is important to understand what form of contribution we have made so far, what our pattern of enabling and our pattern of preventing ourselves from serving the world to our full potential has been. I believe it is important to understand the role of the mind in structuring and evaluating experience. The process of generating deeper awareness about ourselves, about interdependence and reciprocity, and ultimately the nature of reality is a prerequisite for contributing to wholeness rather than fragmentation. You might have begun to accept that straightforward paths are the exceptions and your leadership journey meanders. You might have discovered the cure that is awareness. When our mind begins to gain freedom from being simply reactionary, we can overcome the patterns that limit us. The freer the mind, the more it turns toward the whole. It

CHAPTER FIVE: CONTRIBUTION

encompasses experience with compassion, not only other people's experience but also our own, and it gradually realizes that our most ingrained habit, the attachment to ourselves and the images we create around the self, is likely to limit our contribution to life. Transcending experience and becoming more aware makes our place in the world become more relative, less grand, less assertive, but more responsive. With rising awareness we feel more at home in the Universe, realizing that we are not alone and that we are part of a collective journey. We can actually integrate all experiences and the fragmented parts of ourselves. Understanding that our fears are mirrors of fragmentation helps to bring the underlying forces that are informing and influencing our leadership journey to the surface. We find our voice in a more authentic way and we are led into our true potential to contribute. Finding our particular rhythm becomes a helpful inner space for our generative capacity. It is healing when we can embrace our early intention without disregarding it for its naivety. We can see the essentially human values it held and can integrate it into our future contribution in a mature way.

Walter has worked for a large pharmaceutical company in the United States for a long time. As a deeply religious person, his life and leadership journey has been inspired by deeper values. However, the reality in the company didn't always match his inner need for value-based leadership. Recently he became a diversity manager and more confident to do what he really wanted to do:

> If I had to define what I've wanted to bring into the world at different times it is a resounding shout that says, 'Hey, let's slow down for just a minute and look around. Shouldn't we be spending more thought and energy on understanding the elements of human connectedness (or lack thereof)? Isn't it people who make things happen? Isn't it possible that we could all benefit from understanding each other better and

appreciating what we each have to share? Aside from our cultural, ethnic, religious and gender differences, could we benefit by exploring how much commonality we have in what really matters in life (i. e. our loved ones, security/safety, having what we need to sustain and enhance life, getting along, creating new opportunities, providing opportunities for our children, etc.) even though we may choose to express these wants/needs in different ways?

The result of all the changes in our transformative process can be a shift in the inner ground from which we lead. This might happen so subtly that we do not notice it at the time. Uncovering our own humanity is a road with no final destination but progressive clarity. When our inner field changes, we will notice changes in the outer field. Different things happen, we meet different people. Our driving force will become the intention to serve rather than a need for recognition. We might reconnect with passion nourished by compassion for the world and humankind; we will hold our commitment as a feeling of freedom of responsibility, in the awareness of the inseparability of choice and necessity. We might gradually cultivate reflection in action, knowing that the space inside us is not really separate from the outside world.

A Glimpse into Theory: Identity and Accountability

An important feature of living systems is that they continuously try to create a dynamic balance between the two tendencies of self-assertion and integration. Overemphasis of one and neglect of the other leads to imbalance, usually endangering the system in one way or another (Capra, 1996, p. 9). Self-interest, in this view, is not morally bad. It is a healthy aspect of the maintenance of systems. Only when it is not contained and modified in dialogue with others, or other levels of the whole, does it become detrimental to others, the whole, and eventually itself. Hence, a dynamic balance in nature always works as a balance between self-interest and interests beyond the self (Sahtouris & Lovelock, 2000, p. 280). We live with the construct of our separate self because we can perceive the form and matter of our individuality. Indeed, we do have a history that is different from somebody else's history, and a composition of mind structured by our personal experience in its particular form (Fleischmann, 1999, p. 133). But any worship of the doctrine of the soul, a particular purpose for us or our need to respond to a call is probably illusive and prevents us from paying attention to a larger context. The emphasis is not on our particular call and purpose, but on being able to sense both the requirements and the possibilities of the larger whole and attend to it. In her discussions on the illusion of self, Joanna Macy quotes Ralph Wendell Burhoe: 'A comprehensive view reveals no such thing as a personal self-actualization apart from a self's role or the self's niche in a larger ecosystem of civilization and biosphere. The vision of an independent self to be fulfilled is a lethal mirage ... Our civilization has failed the individual in failing to infuse him with an understanding of the larger dimension of self as the servant of ... a larger ecosystem' (in Macy, 1991a). Although our path is at no point predetermined and choice is always open to us, we are inseparable from the world and our function in the larger ecosystem. Our leadership journey can thus never be value-free, the 'how' of being a leader can never be independent from the 'what'. In such a perspective, the over-emphasis on individuality and the exclusive insistence on free will is as illusive as the construct of 'self'. All of it exists, but as part of an interconnected nature of reality. The notion of accountability or responsibility in the understanding of identity is often related to a humanly created societal or religious or political set of values, which in themselves are changeable and intertwined with history and the respective mindset. One would expect that a system's view on identity or even a biological view would reveal no such issues as values: nature seems to be value-free. And yet, a glimpse into chaos theory suggests that most of our actions might matter more than we are aware of. Through this kind of lens one would see life, and subsequently human life, as a combination of free choice and lawful determinacy. 'In each moment, our personal life also contains this union of choice and necessity. Though we often feel buffeted by capricious forces, disarray is illusory, and within even the storm is a downdraft of coherence.' (Fleischmann, 1999, p. 127). This does not mean that each of our action's antecedents and consequences can be mapped out in a clear line of cause and effects, but we seem to participate by our action at every moment in an invisible network of cause and effect, not knowing how we affect this network by what we do or don't do. 'Our choices remain our own, within the context of the unhinged and multifarious events of the world, and each of our choices will instantly begin to travel down the lines of cause and effect ... There exists indeterminacy, choice, but our actions organize pre-existing disarray into magnetic fields of effects. All moments and spaces of freedom are contiguous with vectors of consequence.' (ibid., p. 128).

The impacts of our choices affect us reciprocally, directly or indirectly, in this time or other times. The gift of the human condition is that we can become aware of our choices. When we accept this reciprocal connection between our 'being', our self or identity and our action in the world, the issue of responsibility and accountability as a leader is not just a noble gesture, a compliance with a moral or normative demand, it becomes a pragmatic necessity (Macy 1991b). At first glance this idea is uncomfortable – such a view on identity and responsibility seems to be morally coloured, open to interpretation about what it is that is to be done 'right' or 'wrong'. And indeed, there is considerable evidence in human history of the arrival and departure of values and moral conduct in accordance with prevailing epistemology and ontology. The Buddhist view of causation is different. It suggests a form of accountability towards the life process that cannot be captured by values or moral prescriptions. In Buddhist theory, this is captured by the concept of *karma* (often misunderstood as determination causing fatalism) that provides an understanding of accountability. In broad terms, one could say that karma describes the origin of our identity and personality – a constantly changing and, while changed, partly maintained pattern of forces, mental and bodily actions, beliefs, values, feelings, predispositions and reactions, a constant becoming in an intertwined flow of action and reaction (Fleischmann, 1999, p. 114), a product of the causal process determined by both our own unchangeable history and our new choices. The notion of causality provides a challenging insight into the process of life (Macy, 1991a, p. 170). The real treasure in the concept of karma lies in the insight into the interdependence between choice and necessity. Buddha's insight into the causality of the process of becoming reveals that overcoming our ignorance towards this process of causation leads to the ability to make choices that influence the very process of causation: karma can be changed and so that changes our future karma. The antecedent of choice is intention and motivation. In Buddhist theory, intention as a volition of the mind is seen as very important and choice as a result of it is valued as having such determinative effect that '... the opportunity provided by human existence is considered in the Buddhist view to be incomparably precious ... only the human being can affect experience by choice. The power to determine one's fate is the prerogative of the human realm; and given the astronomical number of other forms of life, this human opportunity is extraordinarily rare and valuable' (Macy, 1991a, p. 173).

If identity is the construct of past action and thought, it is at the same time the engine of intention, motivation and choice of present and future action and thinking. We cannot predict the outcome of each of our choices and actions, but we can become aware and increasingly predictive about the results of our continuous efforts in a certain direction. 'Freedom is the presence, not the absence, of constraints that give ongoing impact and importance to our choices.' (Fleischmann, 1999, p. 129). While nobody can alter previously made choices and their effects, human identity remains a choice-maker in constant flux. It is affected by the past, but, through increasing awareness, it can also break free from the past.

Even though it might happen in small steps, we can influence the course of our own and the world's evolution. Mindfulness lies at the centre of our growing ability to be attentive to what needs doing. I believe that we all have a natural tendency to serve the world. We might not be constantly aware of this, but when we come across a purpose that seems to be worth pursuing, we act on it with a dif-

CHAPTER FIVE: CONTRIBUTION

ferent kind of energy. Our heart engages and we feel more whole. Many change programmes in companies are based on aligning people with a goal that is made worth achieving. They tap into this natural desire to be part of a larger purpose. It is known that people who see meaning in their organizational endeavours work and lead with more inner resourcefulness. But if what we serve is not big enough, not really aligned with our heart or too short-sighted for our heart's intuition, we will perform well, possibly commit, but our hearts won't be in it.

When Gerard began to track important features of his leadership journey he noticed that for certain periods of his career he felt a profound emptiness, although he performed well in the company according to all standards:

> If I look at the work environment and I ask myself, whom did I serve, it was myself, absolutely myself. I was doing this or that, because I had been asked to do it, and I was doing a good job, but it was not for the sake of doing a good job that would help others, it was because it would put me in a very good light and it would help me progress. So that was very prevalent – myself. Also the team members I worked closely with were acting quite similarly. Whatever the business unit was doing, I wasn't really serving that at all. However, I was definitely paying lip-service to it. I designed a strategy for the business unit, but it was truly lip-service, and ultimately I became very uneasy not being able to serve the larger context. Because I didn't want to serve my boss and my boss's boss, because I knew they were only serving themselves. There was no way that I could align with that. If what I serve is not big enough I lack passion.

Real service needs the engagement of the heart. It also needs an open and self-reflective identity. Expansion of the humility that naturally results from mindfulness is the basis of a serving contribution that serves the world as well as ourselves. If our outer service and our inner development of awareness are misaligned, our contribution might be far from beneficial in the long run. We can come to the rational conclusion that we want to redefine our leadership contribution and map out our path towards more sustainable leadership action. But if we have not tracked our own path and understood the patterns that hold our identity in place, we might move into the new with the old strings still attached. The new course might then lack the clarity we long for or we might begin to be and act differently with no resonance from our surroundings. If you consider redefining your leadership contribution the past needs to be resolved – not overcome, not cleared, but understood, accepted and valued. *Without genuine compassion for yourself and the detours you took on your road you will not be able to act from the deeper field within that resonates with the whole.* Leading in favour of humankind and a sustainable world requires our own humanity. We become more human as we become more mindful of who we are and how we have come to be. When we become compassionate we cannot *not* radiate who we are – it flows by itself.

As with other aspects of your journey, there is a pattern to your questioning your leadership contribution that is worth noticing. The shift in your heart comes in small steps. The cases in which leaders suddenly break with the past and start on something new that engages their heart and their willingness to serve are rare. For most of us there is already a history of reconsidering our contribution that we may have ignored for some time. It shows itself in repetitive thoughts or feelings that we want to engage in something that lies too far away from our current reality, or we do not know what to do to make it happen. It shows itself in an idea we have that we might not have told anybody because we are afraid of being ridiculed. It shows itself in our insecurity about our capacity to contribute.

CHAPTER FIVE: CONTRIBUTION

Mandy's deeper intention has always been about voice, her own and others'. This deeper desire to heal through voice has accompanied her throughout her leadership journey and has unconsciously informed many of her choices:

> If you had asked me what I would do if there where no constraints on me and I could freely choose, I knew what I would do. I asked myself this a number of times. I know it. But it would take a lot of guts for me to say it and do it. I would go a thousand different ways to find people who might be interested in allowing me to help in places where there is deep conflict or there is real pain in the world, or where people are driven apart by difficult history like in Northern Ireland. I have hardly ever talked about this wish of mine; I hardly ever gave voice to this, because I think who am I to help here? But if you asked not whether I would feel capable, but what I wanted to do, that's what I wanted to do. It would, for example, be working with children who had been torn away from their family, or disenfranchised people. It would be about allowing those voices to be 'up and out' so that they could find the space where it is acceptable for all the voices to have their say. This could be places where there is deep political unrest, deep social unrest or injustice. It would be a place where there is deep pain and where people have lost the ability to make sense of each other. It would not be about making money. It would be about helping other people to speak for themselves. It is not that I hold the belief that this is all that is needed, I know there is much more to it. But what I wanted to contribute is something that has to do with voice and tone. I have held the picture that where there is deep pain and deep division, and a sense of futility about the way forward, there is something about the nature of voice and tone

that is healing as opposed to divisive. I don't know what to do with this insight, but that is what I would want to do.

There is a red thread running throughout our leadership journey. It connects our early intention with the quest of our heart, the way we chart our leadership journey and our slow and contemplative response to the question of what we would do if we had no constraints, no financial obligations. The further away the response is from what we are doing today, the louder the invitation to think and track our journey. We remember this – the world did not necessarily embrace our early intention. We got blocked, people did not understand, we learned to tuck it away and become more 'realistic'. The same might happen to the response to the question of what we would do if we had no constraints. This time it is not only the world that that might laugh at us. We have internalized the impossibility of our intention's implementation. We do not even talk about it. We lack trust in our ability to manifest our contribution. We know it is simply impossible to implement because the circumstances do not allow it. But I believe it is worth holding on to – not that we can expect to implement it exactly the way it is held in our mind. But if we feel our heart's longing combined with what we feel needs doing in the world, this is an indicator of the depth of our potential contribution. It is time to accept that it is there and to attend to it. This does not mean that we need to change our life radically between today and tomorrow. It means that we consciously decide to let our intention mature. We do not need to give it a predefined form. It might never take on the exact manifestation we have in mind. But we can create a space for it to ripen over time. When we get to the essence of it we can begin to ask different question – *how would we lead, if we were led by our intention? What would change?*

Samson still lives in Ethiopia and his country is still governed by forces that do not allow much opposition. Life under such cir-

CHAPTER FIVE: CONTRIBUTION

cumstances is unpredictable, security and peace are volatile, but he has not given up on his belief that the world can become a different place. Time and his professional work allowed him to experience that connecting beyond the limitations of one nation can be a gateway to world consciousness:

> If money was not an issue I would devote myself more and more to understanding the world and to writing down my observations. Do you remember when we had our dialogue in Chipping Camden, in the middle of England, around the idea of forming sustainable patterns in the world that would work? Do you remember how I, noticeably from Ethiopia, said: 'I belong here in England as much as I belong in Ethiopia. We might not be aware of it but we all belong. We are all in the same boat. Do we feel that? And what would change if we did?' I would like to know more about it and there would be something I would do workwise to put this in writing. This is what I would do.

Rethinking your contribution can take time. It is not something that reveals itself in an instant. But if you are prepared to listen, you will find thoughts, ideas, desires and dreams. They all have something familiar. You do not re-invent yourself – you are reconnecting with your own story. Attending to this requires courage. It requires courage to track your journey and face your potentials and your limitations, and courage to venture into the unknown and to look at your fears. There is no guarantee of success. You will not know how the world will respond to your revised contribution. You will need perseverance. Do not be surprised if you face vagueness for a long time. Redefining your leadership contribution is a process of maturation. It cannot be forced. Its character and speed is different for each of us. What I am suggesting is that it is worthwhile for

CHAPTER FIVE: CONTRIBUTION

each of us to ponder the question: what is my contribution to what needs doing in the world? How do I want to live that contribution considering my unique potential and what the world needs?

When Edith finally decided to settle in South Africa, she had found the place where she thought her experience and her longing to contribute could crystallize in a way that would support the transformation of the country. Her choice reflected the consistent quest for equality and tolerance she had felt throughout her leadership journey. She created a foundation in support of black businesswomen:

> What I am doing now, is taking small steps. To be honest, sometimes I would love to be militant, and break rules, stand on the podium and really fire people up and reach the masses on women's rights. My focus is and always has been on respect for women. If women's energy does not become a more active part of the world's course, the nurturing is missing, healing is missing, and so is laughter. I think women need to take a leadership role to get the balance right.

Edith found a way of integrating her experience in international business with her desire to foster women and to contribute to the healing of a fragmented society. But what sounded straightforward to begin with has turned into a long journey. Edith needed the perseverance, patience and clarity of vision that she had trained herself in when she was in the world of international telecommunication businesses. Her experience there was of utmost importance for the redefinition of her contribution. Although she moved contexts, she did not need to abandon her skills:

> For me, having this vision of making a different contribution meant that I was in a place that was no longer good enough.

CHAPTER FIVE: CONTRIBUTION

And then came the time of turmoil and struggle, the search for and loss of orientation. I always had an image that helped me – I thought of a kind of friction area, of which one part is the familiar one I am willing to leave, and the other part is a no-man's-land, a scary place to go. When you are in between, there are all the old habits that anchor you in the old world but the vision and the passion are in the new world – there is a strong energy that pulls you towards the new, even if large parts of it are unknown to you. If one has courage and curiosity, one can win the inner battle; if one is fearful, one will certainly fail. Then the actual intention gets compromised and suppressed.

Intention creates energy fields. It organizes life. It creates order in our path, it attracts people and opportunities. When we neglect our deeper intention it withers and we fall short of our potential. We might not need grand visions; in fact, we sometimes prevent ourselves from changing by building visions that are so grand that we are overwhelmed by their presence. We cannot expect that our intention will always be crystal clear. But we know that we have come closer to ourselves when the voices outside of us become less influential, less forceful. The cost of non-compliance with the demands of the world we have constructed for ourselves becomes less important. When we have come to know our own story, we are more able to sustain our new-found confidence. We gain an inner freedom from conventions, from the need for recognition, and from structures that have restricted us. We begin to dance to our own tune, which is the tune of a larger underlying story. *In this story, tending the common is not an additional voluntary service, but the deeper meaning of our being here.*

It is not that Philele did not enjoy his influential position in the South African government. He felt fully accountable to the course his ministry was going to take. But there was something about the use of status he observed among his colleagues that he deeply disliked. He noticed how the seduction of power and material wealth trapped people in their egos and drew a lot of energy away from the actual task – serving the communities. He also felt how he slowly became removed from the direct support for people; how his status began to draw dividing lines between him and the people on the ground. He noticed how his old passion resurfaced – empowering people. Finally he began to experiment with entering new settings that allowed him to develop different aspects of his leadership identity. In addition to his managerial task he began to facilitate leadership development courses:

> I tend to want to revolve around concrete help for people to improve their lives and one of the things is this work of facilitating these courses around actually very practical issues. It is quite refreshing to find myself interacting with people and seeing how they organize their lives and I contribute resources, the value of the network that I have. Sometimes I can help in resolving what may be almost impossible for them to resolve themselves because they may not be properly linked to what they need. I find myself enjoying that sort of work when I can contribute to improving people's lives. It links to my old question of justice. This work of facilitating, helping others to work among themselves more effectively, is the kind of work that I really enjoy and would like to do more of.

When internal volition moves you towards redefining your leadership contribution, the hardest thing to accept is that it might take time before this finds a form with which you feel entirely at home. There might be people for whom the redefined contribution is clear from the start, but there may be many more of us for whom

CHAPTER FIVE: CONTRIBUTION

a search with an unpredictable outcome begins. Expect vagueness in the beginning. Something that has been lying dormant cannot take shape quickly. A learning process is starting, which takes its own particular course. The most important inner attitude on the new journey is twofold – to be open to learning and new encounters, and to be willing to try something out knowing it might not be the final answer.

When I stopped working for a large development cooperation company I did so because I had known for a considerable amount of time that my contribution had been lost at a certain point. I had had a remarkable career in the company with opportunities I considered fortunate – until I hit the resistance of a new superior who I perceived as intending to subtly but noticeably tame my free spirit. I tried various ways to win back lost ground and one part of me wanted to stay in the company, very much attracted by the financial security it had to offer. It took me almost two years before I finally knew that I had to leave to revive my heart's desire. When I had almost made up my mind and begun to plan my exit, I was offered work I could only dream of at a company in the United States. It felt very much as if life was supporting my move. Not only did the new contract enable me to quit my old job, but at the centre of my new work were all the values that I had so desperately tried to integrate into my previous job. It felt as if I had found my destination – a family of like-minded people. But life offers opportunities and moves on. Only a year later I realized that what had felt like home was not *my* home. Rather, it was an important stage in a process of unknown outcome. I was grateful to have experienced this time, in which many foundations for my future work were laid. But it was not the destination; it equipped me to begin the search for my real leadership contribution.

Redefining your leadership contribution does not free you from the messiness of life. But it encourages you to accept messiness as part of the journey. In the beginning there is often loneliness, particularly when you live or work in an environment where you cannot talk about the process of change within you or feel that people would begin to understand the significance of questioning your leadership contribution. So solitude is an unavoidable feature of the process. You might feel like you're living in a desert or that you've been born into the wrong family. The feeling of alienation is widespread among leaders who begin to search for a more meaningful contribution. It often helps to talk to entirely different people about what is happening. It might help to get a coach who understands leadership beyond its performance aspect. Above all, it helps to accept the solitude as part of the process.

On a deeper level, you might not be alone – many more leaders, even those around you who you cannot imagine might understand your journey, have a deeper intention to contribute. But they might be at a different stage of their journey. That is where reconnecting with your young leadership story and your deeper initial intention is important. It gives you the thread you can hold onto in times of doubt and difficulty. You need to place your trust in this storyline to be able to try out a new path, a new behaviour, a new activity, without the immediate fear of failure. Disappointments are part of the deal. Expect them without giving them too much weight. You are on a learning road. The redefinition of your leadership contribution will be built from successes and failures. Life has its own way of teaching.

When Lesley went through a strange encounter in which her team challenged her leadership capabilities (as a team leader in organizational change), she knew she had to leave the multinational bank and find a new path. She asked for a sabbatical during which she worked part-time in a young consultancy company that espoused the very values she had been missing in the bank – a dialogic way of shaping the future in organizations. This was at the core of her deepest intention – helping people find a voice when they don't have a voice:

> What I have always found very attractive is something around advocacy, ensuring that people get heard, people who are affected by big organizations and government. It is about preventing unfairness from happening. I don't yet know what it is that I will do on my new path, I can't hunt it down. I need to try things out and see what comes next, and find the balance between my active search and waiting for it to emerge – the place where I can apply my skills in a different form. Dialogue work attracts me because through dialogue people can be heard, and can express their thoughts, concerns and aspirations. This can help a group of people move into a more meaningful expression of their potential.

Lesley finally helped to build the consultancy, only to learn over time that the espoused values of her colleagues were not always the lived values. A year later she left the company very disappointed when she had realized it was not her new home. It had been an invaluable experience for her journey, a remarkable learning step enriching her ability to create settings in businesses in which people could open up to deeper questions. But she had to move on, faithful to her journey. Equipped with such experience she continued the search towards redefining her leadership contribution.

You can embark on the process of redefining your leadership contribution within the professional setting you are working in or by leaving it, taking time off and reshaping your professional path. Probably the most common feature is that enlightenment, clarity and fulfilment do not arrive immediately. On the contrary, we might need to put up with the arduous work of gradually gaining clarity about the form and shape of our future contribution. This might sound disheartening. We might believe that because we have needed so much courage to break the old patterns, reconnect with our intention and actually take the first steps into the unknown, that we deserve a positive response from life and other people. We need encouragement. I believe when we listen attentively, we receive it. It is a matter of being alert not only to the loud feedback life is providing but to the many subtle undertones, friendly remarks, supportive questions, and shy encouragements.

When Gerard left the multinational company, giving up splendid career opportunities for a one-year sabbatical, he heard the annoying rumour that something in his performance must have caused the company to make him leave – this was the only way some colleagues could cope with his challenging move. But many fellow leaders came to him privately, not only to wish him well, but to express their wish they had the courage to do the same.

There is always encouragement – we simply need to hear it and take it seriously. And we need to take our heart's desire seriously. Waiting for the great call might trap us in our ego's desire to be chosen. It is fine to battle with the vagueness of our new journey – this means we are happily on our way. We can keep track of our feelings of meaninglessness and our deeper desire to contribute. We can notice that success, power and money are sometimes fake substitutes for what we are really looking for – the sense of participating in the evolutionary process in a way that helps, furthers life and brings about a more sustainable future for all. When we begin to redefine our leadership contribution, it is worth holding onto our ideals – not so tightly that they cannot be shaped by experience, but tightly enough not to be tossed around in the storms of an unknown path. Gradually, we will become confident that we can grow into our larger potential. With all our gifts and experience, we do have the capacity to manifest possibilities of life that would otherwise not come into being. Our choices count. We can

CHAPTER FIVE: CONTRIBUTION

influence the manifestation of reality. Life is transitory, but in no way meaningless. There are infinite possibilities in every moment, many of which never actualize. The evolutionary process depends on our choices, and on our growing awareness about our capacity to enact life-sustaining possibilities.

Doris started a promising career at one of the largest German car manufactures. With a brilliant university business degree behind her, and fluent in English, French and German, her ambition for an accelerated career path was supported by her superiors. At the age of 27, their faith in her abilities paid off – she managed a satellite marketing department of the company in the US very successfully. When she moved to her next job back in her home country, obstacles suddenly began to crop up. Her boss resented that her abilities were more recognized in the hierarchy above him than his own. He began to block her path. Doris found her way out of the crisis, but did not feel the same satisfaction in her job anymore. Doubts set in. There seemed to be more to life than careers and cars. She felt a loss of orientation and an absence of meaning. Slowly she began the search for her new contribution. She discovered that there was a whole world out there she had rarely had access to – people working towards a better future in developing countries. Finally, she negotiated a sabbatical and volunteered to work on UN development projects. New contacts opened up new opportunities and everything seemed to click into place when a large donor agency offered her a post designed to foster co-operation between development aid and private companies' engagement in developing countries. She happily agreed to take the post, only to experience the most difficult year of her professional life. With all her fresh enthusiasm and brilliant ideas, she hit an entirely different organizational culture. Nobody had warned her about the staff's misgivings about private companies in development projects. Her inability to influence the situation

CHAPTER FIVE: CONTRIBUTION

positively contradicted the professional experience she had had in business. She battled her way through, but it gradually became clear that this was not the fulfilment she had hoped for. She knew that the actual content of her new direction was correct. Even though her old identity attracted her because it seemed to promise easier rewards, she decided to remain faithful to her new direction. When the contract at the donor agency came to an end she did not ask for a renewal, but decided to freelance in the area in which she had begun to develop her special competency: partnerships for sustainable development. Again, life responded to her heart's desire. She found like-minded people and began to build a new organization.

When we feel our heart calling we must act on it. Nothing undermines our deeper intention more than the continual postponement of decisive action. When we feed our own inertia and reticence we drain the life force embedded in our deeper intention. There is a time to wait while things come into being and there is a time to act. Knowing the difference can be developed by tracking our journey, reconnecting with our early journey and testing our new path. We need to make moves without a safety net. This is often easier said than done. But I believe that even when we depend on our secure income there are moves to make that can ensure the engagement of our heart and faithfulness to our intention.

What makes Diane stay in the multinational company is the vision she had no matter how far it seemed, of coming closer to the work she actually wanted to do:

> If I was independently wealthy, the type of work I would be doing is almost what I do now, probably not exactly in the area that I am in, but in principle the type of work that I am doing now. I see a tremendous need, specifically in large corporations, to become more aware of their responsibility in

CHAPTER FIVE: CONTRIBUTION

the world. I want to help people to see how they are part of a large connected system. Connection and accountability – that is work that attracts me and always has.

Redefining our leadership journey does not always mean that we need to leave our jobs or break with our current career path. It may mean a simple adjustment. More and more companies are calling for people who bring in experiences that can help those companies to build their roles as corporate citizens. The nature and tradition of large companies may inherently treat such people ambivalently. But with the growing concern for humanity's future, the opportunities for developing responsible business action will also grow. No matter how many setbacks there are to issues of poverty reduction and sustainability for our planet, slowly but surely the role of businesses will have to change, and governments will become more responsive learning entities. No contribution to a more sustainable world is too small.

Lucia had her doubts about some of the leaders in her company, but she thoroughly believed that no matter how the history of the company had developed there was potential to become a responsible global citizen:

> I want to serve an organization not an individual. But then 'the organization', what does that mean? Does that mean shareholders' values? Of course, it doesn't. So for me the step beyond organization is society. In my case, the challenge is fascinating and at the same time frightening. How can we solve the paradox of providing mobility, transport, heat, light and everything else, power and electricity, and provide that to society without polluting or destroying the environment? It would need developing a socioeconomic position of the company far beyond what has been the case in the past.

> Hydrocarbons are normally found in developing countries with sometimes corrupt governments and a very, very needy poor population, and how do we resolve that? There are massive kinds of things that I can feel I can contribute to. And there are small steps to be taken collectively. That to me is really exciting. Ultimately, when we get this right we serve society.

When we redefine our leadership contribution within an existing career path, we will be attracted to the old ways of generating success and rewards. It helps to observe how this happens and whether it supports the new contribution or delays it. The new path needs attention. If we neglect it and continue to thrive on the old, we prevent our heart's engagement. It takes courage to risk a working pattern of success or a promise of power and influence. But the redefinition of our leadership contribution requires nourishment and nurturing. We need to fence in our search for a new contribution like we would a small plant. This way it can grow in peace and become resilient enough to weather the first storms. It is important to bear in mind that the first steps on a new path are always experimental and should be viewed that way. If we expect the first change to be the final destination, we will encounter severe periods of disappointment. We might not be able to avoid disappointment anyway. Remember – the world did not respond with excitement to our early intention. This might happen again. But we do not need to feed into our own disappointment by nourishing our sense of grandiosity or idealizing people who seem to be enlightened already. We are all human. We can walk a path together and learn through feedback. Humility is the best companion of all.

When we begin walking a new path it is tremendously helpful to understand our own storyline. We have come to be the way we are in a certain way and this has affected how we made sense of our

CHAPTER FIVE: CONTRIBUTION

experiences. If we know our patterns we know they will accompany us while we slowly begin to change them, even if only by observing them. Sometimes old patterns hold us in place. We abuse our body and mind by overworking. We avoid reflection. We hide from real commitment because we believe that it would constrain our freedom. We are not saints and we will not become saints as a result of redefining our leadership journey. Reconnecting with our early intention means we simply follow our natural tendency – to serve life by applying our unique abilities. No matter what stage we are at in life, we have matured through experience and can use that to foster our new path. We notice that something has shifted internally when the hesitation is over. We can then accept that rethinking our leadership contribution will not have a predictable outcome. There is no fixed solution to what is inherently designed as a learning process. We might get better at adjusting to what is needed. But we cannot attach a timeframe to it. The road becomes visible in front of us, but we cannot see beyond the horizon. There is one clear indication marking an internal shift – when there is *no longer anxiety about succeeding*. When this happens we walk the path with increasing inner serenity. This doesn't mean that we won't face difficulties – there will be times when we do not know how to continue. But our inner ground of leading has shifted. This is the moment when fear of failure is not a guiding force anymore, because failure is just one aspect of the learning process. Because we have reconciled with our own journey we do not need to block out the feedback life and people are giving us. This is fertile ground for sustainability leadership. We enter the great dance with no need to hold tightly to what we have begun to do and no need to defend who we believe we are. We can listen from beyond ourselves. When the inner ground of our leadership contribution shifts, fears seem to disappear. The inner focus of serving seems to lessen the need to assert the self. As a result we feel more at ease, and more at home in the world. Leading from this inner ground is not about radiating greatness and excelling over others or getting recognition and reward. It is not even the superficial enjoyment of influence. It is the humble experience of gladness at being able to contribute.

The meaning of power changes and so does the role of influence. Both aspects are important. There is no hope of leading towards a more sustainable world if we do not bring our influence to bear. But influence does not serve our own feelings of greatness anymore. It serves a purpose beyond ourselves and when we have laid out a network of feedback, we have at least taken serious steps to welcome learning.

Mandy summarized the essence of this inner attitude:

> When I am really holding myself in a clear commitment to serving life and others, my awareness and connection to life is much deeper and much stronger. All of the worry about what to do next just disappears.

When we generate deeper awareness about ourselves, about interdependence and reciprocity, we understand more about the nature of reality. In the transcendence of our experiences we gain more inner freedom and overcome our own limiting patterns. This helps us on the new path. The freer the mind the more it becomes concerned with the whole.

As the shifting ground inside us becomes more stable, we begin to see reality in a different way. Where before we saw people competing with us or people we never really understood, we now begin to see other people's journeys. One of the most striking realizations is that we are not travelling alone. We sense the innumerable fellow travellers with quests, intentions that live and get lost and are found again, and a deep unanswered desire to serve humanity. We notice the profound discrepancies between people's deeper desires and the

CHAPTER FIVE: CONTRIBUTION

more visible level of corporate action. We see performance orientation disconnected from the heart, the rigidity and constraints in the focus on shareholder values only and the internal politics in organizations as journeys that have gone astray. We do not know how many faces conceal similar longings, the same unanswered questions, or a like-minded journey. This is probably the most common feature – when we decide to change our journey towards more meaningful contribution our urge to come home grows. This can take many different forms. As we reconnect with our storyline and become more and more who we really are, less fragmented, less tortured by the defence of a certain identity, we feel the need to connect and reconnect on many different levels. For some of us the desire to reconnect with our inner core, often reflected in where we are coming from, might have a geographical dimension.

When Gerard took a year off he went back with his wife and two children to the place in France where they had lived before he had begun to frequently change jobs and, subsequently, places, as part of his career within the multinational company. The familiar feeling of being close to nature that was at the very core of his early journey helped him to access the deeper layers of his personality: the longing for harmony that had been buried under his career advancements.

As my ideas about my future contribution gradually took shape and I knew that I would begin to build an institute dedicated to sustainability leadership, I quite rationally considered Berlin to be a good location to establish the Institute. I talked to many people to get their views on this, until I finally knew that, apart from all the strategic considerations, there was a part of me that wanted to be home. It took time to listen to the longing, but I finally found myself settling not more than a few kilometres away from the place where I had my early dreams. Only now I had crossed the now non-existent border and had found my place in the river landscape so familiar to my heart in what had formerly been East Germany.

CHAPTER FIVE: CONTRIBUTION

Redefining your leadership contribution is also a journey home. Such journeys are inspired by longing. This doesn't mean that everyone needs to move or settle in the place of their upbringing. There are different ways of finding home. But the search for a place that feels like home, be it geographical, mental or community-related, is inadvertently part of the journey. It helps to be aware of this. At this point, we search for company, for like-minded people or communities of action that we can join.

Mandy realized that even though her consultancy practice was going well, the constant sense of loneliness was a sore point in her journey. She had learned to accept it, but also knew that deep inside her there was a longing for a form of home that would enhance her and other people's journeys:

> I wish I could form a community over time that would create place and space for people to pursue and share their journeys and identify certain similar patterns and similar volitions in the way they want to engage in the world. I wonder how such communities form, how much they need a fixed shape or a strong purpose and intent. I wish I could be part of enabling that without necessarily wanting to have it my way. The desire to be part of a community is a much more important part of my leadership now. I want to be part of creating it, but also be part of serving it, attentive to what comes through that community and be able to allow it to change, whatever direction it seeks to take.

When this point in the journey is reached, a whole new set of questions opens up. They all relate to the theme of leading in conjunction with others. What is my own contribution and what is that of others? How do we interrelate? If the ground from which I lead has shifted, how will it reflect in the collective? What is my role in

CHAPTER FIVE: CONTRIBUTION

collectively leading towards more sustainable action in the world? How can I lead within an organization or among other people with the intention to contribute to a more sustainable world?

This is more than a desire to belong. It is the realization that we are part of a collective space, that we do not bring forth life alone. Hence we can make conscious choices about how and with whom we may want to co-create more consciously. The search for a collective space into which we can bring our gifts is important. I would like to encourage you not to neglect this urge or play it down. Human consciousness has a way of popping up at different places at the same time without obvious connection. Hence it is worth looking out for who is doing what in the areas we feel we might be able to contribute more. Modern technology offers the greatest opportunities for finding out what is going on. But only actual meetings with other people make a difference. It is the person-to-person encounter that changes our thinking and our path. There is no substitute. Conversational encounters bring our individual development back into the world of interdependence where leading is a collective endeavour. While our mind has changed and we search for more suitable outer action, we will experience both inspiration and disillusionment as ingredients of our new leadership contribution. Again, it is useful to know that we are longing for home because as much as this leads us in the right direction, it can also trap us into illusionary expectations. We might join up with a community of people only to experience a harsh landing in reality. People are not perfect. We might find bigotry, espoused but not lived values, betrayal, mistrust or intrigues. It is important to consider that such experiences of disappointment can partly be the result of our own projections. Because we needed to find a new home, we might have idealized people. But human beings are imperfect, sometimes unaware of their impact, ignorant of what they cause. The more we reconcile with our own limitations and with the meandering of our path, the more serene we can be in the light of other people's imperfections. The less we need to cling to a certain image of our identity, the less we will suffer from disappointment. We will know when a home is not a home, when we have to move on and find a more suitable collective endeavour for our redefined leadership contribution. But we will gradually gain the resilience we need to follow our intention. We might find the golden mean between compassion, humility, vision and decisiveness.

As we move towards our new contribution, we need to re-assemble our leadership experiences. Leading for the common good requires that we influence the course of life. We need to apply our leadership capabilities. No past experience needs to be lost. It can all be used. But with the shifted ground from which we lead, different questions emerge – how will we know when we contribute to wholeness? How do we know what will be sustainable?

A Glimpse into Theory: Life Enhancing Centres

The quest for understanding the world as one great whole expressing itself in the vast variety of life is as old as humankind and has often been the subject of religious, philosophical and natural science studies. Particularly, views on the relationship between human beings and nature have evolved through many different paradigms: one such view – which we have all grown up with and internalized to a great extent – was the scientific view on life as isolated, broken down into fragments, in order to understand how it works. The result is the presence of many mechanistic models describing reality. None of these models or paradigms is wrong, but more and more people argue that such a limited approach to the vastness of life not only excludes a broader

CHAPTER FIVE: CONTRIBUTION

view, but is not life-enhancing. We're almost used to a lifeless mechanical reality that we struggle to influence to make it obey to our rules. We are not always successful with this attempt to create the world according to our calculations. Mechanics serve their purpose and are indispensable in many aspects of technological development. But despite all recent ambitious attempts, we cannot create life. It creates itself, while we observe, contribute, but we're never entirely in charge. The architect Christopher Alexander suggests a different worldview – one in which nature's tendency to create wholeness is at the centre. In this view, whatever reality we look at has differing degrees of life-enhancing harmony – the infinite possibilities of structures and their combination have an effect on the world – they nourish life or drain it. We all know this without scientific evidence – when we are happy, what makes us calm, when our heart resonates, when we feel most connected with life, when our humanity expands and when it shrinks. We are intrinsically linked to the order of life within us and around us. We are constantly being created by this order as much as we participate in creating this order. Christopher Alexander encourages us to start observing closely which of these structures within and without are furthering our sense of aliveness and which are diminishing it. We can take this further and ask ourselves when the order we are creating is life-enhancing or life-draining. We can begin to see ourselves as a centre – a structure made of many internal centres and in itself a centre among centres. The scientist and philosopher Alan Watts reminds us that actually experiencing this as a fact is a cornerstone for different action in the world based on a deeper understanding of life. 'Theoretically, many scientists know that the individual is not a skin-encapsulated ego but an organism-environment field. The organism itself is a point at which the field is 'focused', so that each individual is a unique expression of the behaviour of the whole field, which is ultimately the universe itself. But to know this theoretically is not to feel it to be so' (Impromptu lecture for the Social Relations Colloquium at Harvard University on April 12th, 1963).

Our feeling of being alive, whether it is the experience of connectedness, a deeper insight, or the sight of natural or cultural beauty is a function of a pattern of wholeness. Our heart responds to this wholeness in a pattern, a structure, an order, an encounter, an experience – our own internal order resonates with what we see and experience. We feel nourished, supported by life, empowered. If we don't have this feeling for a long time we get drained, fall sick, or become nasty. Life originates from wholeness.

For Christopher Alexander, the key to wholeness is an interdependent and recursive pattern of centres. 'It is useful to understand, from the beginning, that all systems in the world gain their life, in some fashion, from the cooperation and interaction of the living centres they contain, always in a bootstrap configuration, which allows one centre to be propped up by another, so that each one ignites a spark in the one it helps, and that mutual helping creates life in the whole' (Alexander, 2002, p. 134). Initially we might not know how we can contribute to wholeness, but our deeper intention is a sufficient guide for the journey at the beginning. It might even be the very expression of the life-enhancing wholeness we are looking for now. Over time, and with observation, our ability to sense life-enhancing wholeness and appropriate being and action to support it will grow.

CHAPTER FIVE: CONTRIBUTION

Probably the most important indication of profound change is the way we see our own leadership contribution as part of a larger movement towards sustainability in the world. We do need to serve our own growth in the sense that we need to enhance our own potential to contribute. But with a redefined leadership contribution the focus has shifted as our own maturation is embedded in what we aspire to serve. We do not need to enjoy our own greatness, we do not thrive on resonance with our own identity, and neither do we feel dependent on our own success or afraid of our failure. The shift might be so subtle that it is not evident to other people. With more emphasis on enhancing each other's potential we look differently at the creation of life. We can actually support each other's journeys and as we do so we might gradually notice that our own journey grows stronger. Connectivity and interdependence are no longer theoretical constructs. They have a direct bearing on the way we perceive change in our own lives and in our endeavour to lead. Building resonance becomes the cornerstone of our way of influencing. We might have been leading in this way all along – creating relationships, enhancing authenticity in people, listening for what wants to emerge, listening to people, looking for common ground, being open, engaging, creating shared meaning, living empathy. But now the context is different. We are less fragmented and have become more stable in following our path. When we begin to see our part in the evolutionary process we might realize more clearly that leading takes place collectively. This does not free us from taking a stand and knowing where we want to go – but it equips us to stay in dialogue with ourselves, with others and with life.

CHAPTER FIVE: CONTRIBUTION

Reflections:

If you were led by your intention to create wholeness, how would you lead?

What is the pattern of your questioning your leadership contribution?

When do you feel whole? Can you track the history of this feeling?

If you were absolutely true to yourself, what would the next steps on your leadership journey be?

When you lead something in conjunction with others, what makes the collective endeavour successful?

Chapter 5: Summary

- We participate in the unfolding of evolution no matter whether we choose to contribute or withhold our contribution. We can change the world, even if the change is small. When we support each other in contributing, the change grows.
- The process of generating awareness about ourselves, the interdependence of life and its reciprocity is a prerequisite for contributing to wholeness rather than fragmentation.
- There is a natural tendency in all of us to serve the world. How this gets disturbed, hijacked, demotivated or deadened is a matter of storyline and the degree of alienation from our true self.
- When we look closely we can see the patterns of questioning our leadership contribution. They are worth noting. The shift in our heart happens in small steps in a process of maturation that cannot be forced. If we listen carefully we will always find encouragement. It helps to consciously create space for maturation.
- The question 'How would I lead if I was led by my deeper intention?' is a good starting point for sustained inquiry.
- Real service requires the engagement of the heart. It also requires an open and self-reflective identity.
- Redefining our leadership contribution does not free us from the messiness of life, instead it encourages us to accept messiness as part of the journey. Our new contribution requires resilience. We might finally find the golden mean between compassion, humility, vision and decisiveness.
- Leadership for sustainability and the common good requires us to influence life. We need to apply all of our leadership capability. Over time and with observation our ability to sense life-enhancing wholeness and appropriate action will grow. It helps to stay in dialogue with ourselves, with others and with life.

CHAPTER SIX
SUSTAINABILITY

The meeting room is much too small for almost 45 people. It is hot, the tiled floor does not help much, and the ordinary plastic chairs are not particularly comfortable. Little wind is coming through the open door that leads to the street. The occasional car driving past worsens the acoustics in the room. Down the hill is the sea, the vast Atlantic Ocean of Salvador de Bahia in Brazil, the invitation to a swim is ignored. Despite the almost unbearable heat, the group concentrates on a written document that is projected onto the wall. Step by step we work through it – we're all hoping that this very diverse group will finally agree on one single document. The completion of this document would be an important milestone in this ambitious project. Different versions of the document have been under discussion for months – they have been the cause of conflicts and threats. In an attempt to reach an agreement on something that would lay the foundation for continued collaboration of highly diverse international actors, people have been meeting in various constellations for some time now. I am standing in front of the group with the task of guiding the dialogue in such a way that we move forward without losing anybody's contribution. I do not know which way this will go – will the group break apart, or will its common hope for change hold it together? In accompanying, guiding and facilitating this group over the years, I have gained confidence in its ability to re-establish common ground continuously – against all odds, and despite political, economic and cultural differences. I have also come to believe that the commitment to sustainability – once it has outgrown the usual scepticism and doubts – has the quality of resilience. It survives crises and reaches into the latent deeper desire of even the most critical person – the desire to contribute to the common good. In this group, I have encountered the subtle and silent presence of collective responsibility that arises in a group when a joint move into the future is at stake. Despite all the vested interests, the lingering mistrust, the occasional doubt, we did eventually reach an agreement. When my last call for proposals for change was met with silence I knew we had arrived. Everybody knew. The relief erupted in spontaneous applause – we honoured each other; we achieved the almost impossible. And we proved that it is possible to tend the common.

A challenging initiative involving a wide range of people from coffee growers on all the continents to coffee roasters, from workers' unions to government officials, had taken an important step towards more sustainable growing, trading and production of coffee on the world market. A long way still lay ahead. The agreed voluntary code of practice was to be applied by each and every participant in the coffee value chain. Here was a growing community of people who had voluntarily decided to join a movement of sustainable business practices: company representatives, leaders of coffee cooperatives, coffee farmers, researchers, and activists from civil society, presidents of coffee federations, lawyers, and sustainability managers. These were people who would not necessarily talk to one another, they would not get to know each other under normal business circumstances. The initiative for more sustainable coffee production drew people together whose lives and worldviews differed in the extreme. What spark is it that engenders commitment to a strenuous international learning process with an ambitious goal and an unclear outcome?

This initiative showed me that there is indeed a spark that rekindles a latent desire, our initial intention. Suddenly this desire is nourished, inspired, revived and longs for more. It doesn't lay doubts to rest, but it does create resonance with an emerging possibility. As this happens, the energy changes, people become more present, more open. They are more willing to cooperate while respecting one another's differences. When we feel we don't make a

CHAPTER SIX: SUSTAINABILITY

difference anyway, we cut ourselves off from a nourishing life-force; we become more self-centred and much more concerned with our own well-being. But when there is emotional exposure to the possibility of jointly making a difference in the world, we are drawn to it, not without doubts, but with progressive commitment. It is contagious. The seriousness of the endeavour helps us to stay faithful to the path towards sustainability. However, the sustainability initiative in green coffee production is just a tiny drop in the vast ocean of what needs to and can be done towards more sustainable action in the world.

The participants in the coffee initiative would have all agreed that it was a strenuous process, but not only did it make sense to them, it was, at times, an invaluable experience. Back home in their organization they promoted the business value of sustainability engagement, explained the marketing advantages of sustainable coffee, expressed their concerns that this would really benefit small coffee farmers, and presented the benefits of an ambitious public-private development project. But in the meeting room in Salvador de Bahia, and at any other meeting place in the past, there was more to this group than the rational explanation for each stakeholder's participation. Despite all the repeated political fights and contradictory positions, people felt that there was a climate of responsibility for the future with respect for each other at its core. Without anyone officially mentioning it, everyone involved was aware of the responsibility bestowed on them – they could have made this one step towards sustainability fail or succeed. One of the participants summarized:

> There was an atmosphere of commitment that made it impossible to misbehave – you would not withhold your position, but always stay in the collaborative field. You knew that this was a global learning process we are all in together: nothing is fixed, we learn as we go.

CHAPTER SIX: SUSTAINABILITY

Sustainable action is an individual, organizational, societal and global learning process. No level can be skipped. When you have come as far as considering re-defining your leadership contribution, you have become much more aware of your participation in evolution and the possibilities that open to you once your mind is open. You might have begun to see your role as being a partner of evolution rather than a bystander who makes little or no impact on the process. This does not mean that your influence is strong or ever will be. But in consciously joining a learning process towards sustainable action in the world, you can do your part, together with whoever you decide to join or support. Your own humanity grows because you've reconnected with your true potential, and you begin to feel more comfortable when this inner development is reflected in what you contribute to the world. When your maturity reaches a particular point, you are urged from within to align the inner and outer elements of your journey and you begin to take new steps deliberately. Gradually you notice how an inner drive grows that suggests that you make this redefined path your core activity, rather than keep it separate from your main activities. I would like to encourage you to resiliently nourish your deeper intention by becoming engaged in consciously shaping your contribution to sustainability based on your intention, competence and your experiences.

But how do we find out what makes sense? How do we know if our contribution counts? How do we take the first steps?

There is no set of proven instructions for developing the courage to venture into the unknown. But there are helpful guidelines:

- Do not suppress the urge to change yourself, your situation, your contribution. There is no need for radical break-ups, revolutions or sudden changes in activities, but it is important to listen to what your heart tells you – there is a chance to redefine your leadership contribution. Act on the urge, no matter how small your steps are. Be persistent despite the odds and setbacks.

CHAPTER SIX: SUSTAINABILITY

- Know that you need resilience and the willingness to risk some parts of your identity that you're very used to. At this point you cannot know if your redefined leadership contribution will yield the same reputation, acknowledgement and status. Risk it anyway. If you keep your heart engaged and your mind open to feedback, you will notice a subtle shift in values. What was important before might not be important anymore, and new preferences and values will emerge. You cannot transform the old into the new without changing yourself.
- Be humble enough to accept that you are entering a learning process. There are many, many people who have pondered and written about life-enhancing individual and societal behaviour, conscious evolution, constructive co-creation and sustainable action. But be assured that no one knows how all this will work on a global scale. There is no one movement to achieve this, and there is no agreement on what the best path is. But in disagreement and dialogue, there seems to be an evolutionary possibility opening up.
- Begin a conscious search. What do other people do? What has been written about the aspects that interest you? Who is meeting where and when on issues that align with your new journey? There is no need to re-invent the wheel – find out what is happening already in many parts of the world. Accept that you need time to search for the place where your redefined contribution will be of most value. Allow yourself to enter into an experimental phase. Try out what speaks to you, read what inspires you. Do not go down one path too quickly, but design your own research project. Follow up on this, but do not put yourself under pressure. You need to learn, act and mature in congruence.
- Do not demoralize yourself by insisting that the change must be immediate and substantially different to the old. This creates unnecessary blocks and puts you under performance pressure.

For some people, it is best to change context in order to learn and mature. For others, slow and subtle refocusing of what they are already doing is the best method. When you get tangled in wanting to change your life and your leadership contribution, leave the future to the evolutionary process. Embrace the present. What can you, considering the journey you have gone through in reconnecting with your heart's intention, do here and now, in the very situation you are in at the moment? Be aware of the possibilities for change that lie so close to you that you might miss them.

- Value encounters – you might deliberately contact people you want to learn from or be inspired by. This is an important step towards exposure to other people's journeys. But do not have unrealistically high expectations. Value the humanness and imperfect aspects of the people you meet. Notice and honour chance encounters: sometimes they hold hints and pieces of wisdom that you can integrate into your journey. Do not easily dismiss anything that doesn't meet your criteria. Remember: Other people are also journeying, more or less aware, but most often in search of meaning. Rarely is anyone already enlightened.
- Be on the lookout for fellow travellers. This might not always be easy in a corporate environment, but be sure that even in the most rational and pressurizing climate you are still in the midst of human beings with similar searches, aspirations and the desire to contribute. *Any move towards a more sustainable world needs systems of mutual support and learning.* When you have begun to acknowledge your own shortcomings, you have not only seen through your own facade, but have seen the human tendency to build identities that lock us into certain behaviour. Allow yourself to see through them with compassion. I do believe that there is a *deeper initial intention* in all of us, no matter how deeply buried.

CHAPTER SIX: SUSTAINABILITY

A contribution to more sustainable action in the world requires parallel development of our inner resourcefulness, reflection, mindfulness and its expression in the outer world as redefined leadership contribution. The journey within seeks resonance in life-enhancing action. While the inner process can – but must not be – done alone, the outer journey requires collective leadership. When we have come this far, we can sense that there is interdependence between inner changes in consciousness and the development of collective consciousness. We notice imbalances and healing opportunities. Sometimes the inner process of maturation becomes self-centred and does not reflect in outer contribution. Sometimes the outer contribution to sustainability is given with no awareness of the complex net of interdependencies with the inner leadership journey. Sustainable leadership action has more impact when it is grounded in a process of inner transformation. Outer and inner development need one another and have a reciprocal effect – if one is missing, the other is lost or falls short of its potential. Inner maturation is also vital for collective leadership. When it is no longer important who does what and who gets the credit, we can do what needs doing and collectively enjoy the results. Particularly in the area of leadership for sustainability, we know that even the most heroic single leader is not going to make a meaningful difference. Success, in the sense of sustainability, comes from many doing what is needed where they are.

The success of the coffee initiative hinges on the voluntary commitment and pro-active action of many people. Nobody can effectively control the path, and unless they are convinced that this is for their own and others' benefit, they will not engage. Yes, there are substantial business motivations, there are strategic considerations for companies to enhance their corporate responsibility image and there are economic prospects for coffee growers in supplying coffee that is produced in a more sustainable way. But with a realistic view on the opportunity to invite the global coffee market to adhere to agreed production and trading standards, success ultimately lies in the willingness of millions of people to join a community that is committed to sustainability and to seeing the benefits of it. People need to lead towards sustainability at all levels – despite the fact that we still might not know what sustainability is exactly, or what it could mean for us in the future, or how we get there. We can learn from obvious mistakes, we can listen to frightful scenarios and follow hands-on recommendations. But the deeper underlying principles of leadership for sustainability, the ability to be more in resonance with a healthy evolutionary process, the chance to become a more conscious guardian of sustainable development – this all needs to be learnt. We are at the beginning of a process of rising awareness and are taking it seriously. There are no final answers. The many international and local forums show that we have sincerely moved into a global collective learning space. There is a movement of responsible business action, too. There is more awareness of interdependency in the wake of globalization. No one who is talking about issues of sustainability and corporate responsibility in business today is openly ridiculed by their colleagues. We are making progress in consciousness, willingness and attitudes. Some people might argue that it is too slow, but it is enough to gain confidence in humankind's ability to enter into a more conscious evolution.

A Glimpse into Theory: What is Meant by Sustainability?

There are many definitions of sustainability, but the one most known and most often cited is the one going back to the Brundtland report of the World Commission on Environment and Development: 'Sustainable development is development that meets the needs of the present without

CHAPTER SIX: SUSTAINABILITY

compromising the ability of future generations to meet their own needs' (World Commission on Environment and Development, 1987). This definition contains the essence of sustainable development as a reminder to humankind that the planet's resources are exhaustible. Since the time of this report, much has been thought and written about sustainability as a goal to be pursued by modern global society. The term sustainability was inspired by the science of eco-systems, and describes the ability of such a system to maintain its ecological processes and productivity over time. In the beginning, sustainability was viewed from an environmental perspective, but more recent approaches have viewed the social and economic dimensions as being as important as the environmental dimension. Sustainable development therefore stands for long-lasting development in which reasonable economic prosperity, environmental quality and social equity can be achieved in a balanced way. In the corporate world this is usually referred to as the triple bottom line (economic, environmental, social), a new measurement for business performance. Realization of sustainable development would mean an improvement in living conditions for most people in the world and would also ensure that progress is within the limits and capacities of a functioning global ecosystem. When considered seriously, this prospect has wide-reaching consequences, as it cannot spare any actor in global society:

'Despite differences in definitions, perspectives and priorities, sustainability remains a critical challenge for everyone. In general, the problem is this: traditional patterns of industrial and economic activities are no longer viable, but alternative models are not yet developed. The historical trajectory of the industrial West cannot serve as a model for the development of the industrializing countries, but it cannot be discarded entirely. Ecological systems are severely strained by the cumulative effects of past industrialization and can scarcely support added strains due to future patterns of growth, but there are major uncertainties about what must be done and how. In short, the international community as a whole is involved in a global search for new modes of development, new designs for social interaction, and new technologies for meeting evolving needs, wants, and demands.' (Choucri, 1996).

The ideal path to sustainable progress has not yet been mapped out. But over the years the awareness of the need for sustainability has not only grown, it has triggered a change in thinking at many levels. Inspired by the developing concepts on sustainability, the role of business is viewed very differently now. Whereas before it was assumed that it was mainly the national and global political and governance systems that were responsible for caring for the common good, it is now more explicitly acknowledged that business, and in particular multinational businesses, has a similar responsibility. Not all businesses have joined this movement, but increasingly the reputation of a business is enhanced by doing so. Many corporations, however, have already begun to see sustainability issues as part of their core business, even if only because of pressure brought to bear on them by civil society. Not only has the corporate world begun to face the challenges of sustainable development, governments and communities, global organizations and development organizations take part in what is developing into a global learning process with many forums, dialogues, research and publications. There is growing awareness of the role of participation, partnership and stakeholder involvement as a means to reach more effective solutions. Action towards sustainability is on the increase. But much of it is in the testing phase, the number of people committed to sustainability is still far from reaching critical mass, the impact so far is not yet tangible and too many political systems, individual citizens and corporate citizens are still ignorant of the call for action.

There are many ways in which you can lead more consciously for the common good. Not every redefined contribution needs to flow into international sustainability activities, or needs to show up in public. When you have begun to listen to the whole you will notice that it asks for expression and healing in many different ways. It may be the right step to push your company or organization more decisively into sustainable business action and see whether employees feel comfortable with the new path and whether the market responds positively. But it may be just your expressed growing concern for the humanness in your community or direct environment that makes you help fellow travellers to find their individual paths and peace.

Becoming more familiar with the developing concept of sustainability invites us into a global learning journey. This cannot be delegated to a few people – it is everybody's business. It requires creative and collective thinking and needs innovation. Above all, it calls for action and continuous reflection, because we can only learn as we go. It also asks us to acknowledge that we can learn from life. If we want to become mature partners for a more conscious evolution, we can strengthen our resonance with the evolutionary design through integrating what nature's way is teaching us – we can learn from our own path, from the path of humankind, and from understanding the rhythms of life.

How can we contribute to this global learning journey now that we have come this far? Is there an opportunity to connect our redefined leadership contribution to issues of sustainable development? What leadership action is called for?

Real commitment occurs when the heart is involved, when you have connected to a deeper intention that you allow to guide your actions. There is no magic at work, but the fact that your actions are more grounded in intent helps things to come about that would otherwise not happen. Not that obstacle will disappear from your life, but they will be less frightening and frustrating. They are just that, obstacles – opportunities to learn.

Leadership for sustainability needs all three ingredients:

- your resilient commitment to lead into a certain direction collaboratively
- your heartfelt intention grounded in the understanding of your own humanity, and
- a rhythm of individual and collective reflection.

If we open to the idea of interdependency as the concept of sustainability suggests, we understand that developing our own humanity and taking care of the needs of humanity as a whole affect each other mutually. It becomes obvious that part of the global learning journey is to find a way of more consciously co-creating evolutionary processes that are in favour of humankind and the planet as a whole. Sustainability can only take root when a system acknowledges and cultivates individuality (and with that, diversity) as much as it attends to common interests. This sounds like old knowledge, but so far we have failed to find this state of productive balance on a larger scale. And since everything in the world is affected by everything else, it does not really make sense to concentrate on achieving such a state of harmony only for ourselves (although this is definitely a step in the right direction). There is a certain degree of responsibility for all of us to join the learning journey towards sustainability, even if we

CHAPTER SIX: SUSTAINABILITY

decide to concentrate our action at a local level. Globalization has helped us to experience more directly what interdependence means. Climate change is beginning to teach us a harsher lesson. But still, the logic of the societal or organizational systems in which most of us live and work operate as if interdependence is just a theory. It seems to be difficult to integrate this into the daily flow of organizational business. What we might experience more is re-iterated self-interest and disdain for people. Interconnectedness is often undervalued, if not ignored. In this way, our minds and the structures we create are in constant reciprocity. We build societal and organizational settings that help us ignore interdependency and attention to the whole. Part of the learning journey will therefore be to find more mutually supportive ways of being together.

Walter, the diversity manager in a multinational pharmaceutical company, has built his inclusion strategy on the premise that there must be more to diversity than the business case:

> There is nothing wrong with meeting financial goals but it has to happen in a way that you can create relationships along the way that mutually sustain and build you. This would create the same level of outcomes on a sustainable level rather than this huge investment of energy where everybody experiences burnout, and having all these negative repercussions of people leaving the organizations and not feeling valued. Small incremental adjustments that are much more consistent with the cycle of life, I think, are possible.

It requires both interdependent collective energy and difference to create life and to sustain life. Collective does not imply 'sameness'. In fact, it is the opposite. It implies the variety that is required by life to gain balance and sustainability. Fostering diversity in skills, competence, opinions, perspectives, backgrounds, culture, expertise, and so on would be more likely to create sustainable outcomes in the long run. Complex systems in nature are much more stable and resilient than monolithic structures. This may also apply to us. If we patiently integrate the many different aspects of our journey and our identity, we become more rooted in life, and are less likely to be thrown off our path. The more fragmented we feel, the more we find ourselves cut off from knowing what we really can contribute to this world, and so the more insecure we feel. The process of integration and reconnection is built on our own diversity of experience. We gain trust in our ability to contribute more consciously when we have assembled all of who we are, when no parts have to be segregated or suppressed. This is often mirrored in our trust in others. It makes a difference to our leadership. We have less need to have our image of ourselves reaffirmed. The attachment to self can gradually fade away as we overcome anxiety and develop trust in ourselves, in others and in the logic of life.

Anxiety is essentially human. It will never entirely disappear, but if we have learnt to observe and accept, we are no longer captive to it. We know that unconscious anxiety and attachment to the self are inseparable. Latent and unconscious anxiety subtly informs our action and leads into the unsustainable dynamics of self-protection. As we protect the self, it becomes more and more important and we shut off from the awareness of connection with others and the inner experience of being embedded in a larger whole. Self-importance based on anxiety leads to mistrust, which in turn reinforces self-defense, and so on. If we become aware of this vicious cycle, we begin to see with different eyes – a great deal of human behaviour originates in unconscious anxiety and self-defense. Whole ideologies are built on this.

There are usually two ways this unconscious cycle manifests in our behaviour. Both are intertwined with our social set-up and experience. One frequently used road is self-assertiveness, the other

CHAPTER SIX: SUSTAINABILITY

is self-sacrifice. Depending on our own history of social interaction and inner development, we tend to choose one or the other. It is worth reflecting on which road we have taken in the past. When and where, under what circumstances have we resorted to self-assertiveness rather than self-sacrifice, and when was it the other way round? What is our general tendency? Both outer behaviours are based on the protection of an image we have of ourselves. They serve a meaningful purpose and play a vital role in human interaction, although they are not valued equally. The world usually responds to assertiveness with positive recognition. This gives us the feeling of being whole and on the right path. Our anxiety is temporarily allayed, but then we can easily fall prey to the continuous need to protect our status and achievements.

And if the vicious cycle has taken hold too tightly and we have not yet integrated the many fragments of ourselves into the whole that we are, our self-assertiveness might develop into aggression and domination and our self-sacrifice into submission and self-denial. These are both sides of the same coin – an unsustainable form of co-creation that creates winners and losers, victims and aggressors, because both aspects are intrinsically linked. The self-assertive part of ourselves is nourished by the unconscious need for self-protection, while the corresponding part of ourselves supports the self-assertion of others through conscious or unconscious self-denial. Either way, we are captive to our focus on self. As a strongly self-assertive leader, we hold our anxiety at bay by building a self-image of invulnerability. When we withdraw from leadership because of an inherent tendency for self-sacrifice, we protect our self-image through holding back our contribution. Instead of putting ourselves out in the world with all our gifts – which would make us vulnerable and subject to criticism – we withdraw or leave the field to more assertive leaders. Self-sacrifice is no way to overcome attachment to the self. When we shy away from the voice of our heart, a step in the evolutionary process goes missing. Self-assertiveness and self-sacrifice are mutually enacted; they are Siamese twins because in their essence they are rooted in anxiety. But as with all experience there is always the option to transcend.

When we have started a process of integration we can consciously work with the positive assets that underscore both self-assertiveness and self-sacrifice. We need a certain degree of self-assertion to enable our contribution to be heard, and we need a certain degree of self-sacrifice in order to be able to listen to what others express. We need empathy. In the process of reaching out to our own humanity, we will notice that the need for self-defense diminishes. While we reconnect with our early intention and the red thread of intent that runs through our leadership journey, the patterns of self-protection and anxiety will change. When we feel more at home in the Universe the space that used to be filled with anxiety and self-defense is filled with compassion for the world and other people. The question, How can I excel or what will I achieve?' will gradually shift to, 'How can I best contribute to further this process? How can my contribution serve the collective good?'

With closer connection to our own humanity, we also feel closer to the Universe and humankind as a whole. *Forgetfulness of self is a gift we receive on our journey to our own humanity; mindfulness is the gift we learn to give to the world.* It is possible to take a deliberate step into a different and more sustainable pattern of co-creation. When we are no longer captive to our anxiety, we can harvest the positive essence of self-assertiveness and ground it in the inner posture of *contribution*. And we can harvest the positive essence of self-sacrifice and root it in *responsiveness* (see page 248).

A dynamic balance of responsiveness and contribution allows for a more sustainable generative pattern of co-creation. These aspects cannot be separated. Responsiveness without contribution is a refusal of responsibility. Contribution without responsiveness

CHAPTER SIX: SUSTAINABILITY

is likely to be ignorant of the situation and the needs of others and the whole. Both are essential for leadership for sustainability and for the willingness to learn that it requires. The withdrawal of our contribution can stem as much from the pathology of self-protection as domination over others does. The fear of failure, insignificance, and irrelevance, the worry of not being listened to is as much based on anxiety as the need to exert our own grandiosity and intelligence over others. Withholding our contribution is a refusal to open ourselves to responses from the world. Dominating others is a refusal to listen to intelligent diversity and feedback. *Developing the inner posture of responsiveness and contribution is a side effect of increasing mindfulness.* It is generated in a process of gaining awareness of both ourselves and the larger reality in which we are embedded. Contribution and responsiveness mutually reinforce each other, in ourselves but also in the interactions we have with other people. We feel that the atmosphere changes. This form of co-creation is contagious, maybe, because it is the most natural way of bringing forth life. Difference is not ignored but respected in the search for a collectively intelligent path.

Six months after the meeting in Salvador de Bahia, the coffee initiative met to decide on the next step in the process. Again, the sea was not far away, but it was grey with only occasional sunlight breaking through the clouds in a wintery and cold seaside resort in The Netherlands. Some of the participants from the southern hemisphere didn't bring the right clothes. The meeting room was centrally heated, though, and the atmosphere was tense.

It was clear that this project was about to move towards the establishment of a membership organization, and the implementation of the green coffee production standards was close. So the discussions were intense. Everybody seemed to feel the edge of something new being born. With it came excitement and fear. The responsibility put pressure on people, and, to nobody's surprise, the old conflicts of interest between different stakeholder groups emerged. Differences in priorities, political standpoints and worldviews surfaced. There were people who wanted to move forward quickly and others who wanted to have everything thought through before committing to a particular path. People tended to resort to their stakeholder interest. It was the last day of the meeting and I knew that time was running out. I could only trust my experience – this group had learnt *the art of respectfully processing difference into progress*. What could I contribute to progress? What wanted to emerge that I could help come out? As the facilitator of the meeting I decided that very little intervention was needed. The differences obviously needed to emerge first, and once they were acknowledged people would feel safe enough to move towards an agreement that ensured that their concerns had been taken into account. Taking away pressure and allowing space for people to settle into stakeholder opinions seemed to be the best support. I decided to trust this self-organized process. Doing nothing is sometimes the best contribution. A walk on the beach during the long lunch break gave me the opportunity to restore my mind and gave the others the opportunity to find joint paths while maintaining their stakeholder identity. In the afternoon, two of the stakeholder groups came up with a joint proposal. The third was given time to consider the proposal thoroughly and suggested changes. An hour later the agreement was finalized. The foundations for an innovative membership institution for the worldwide coffee community had been laid. It was amazing to experience collective creation as a result of respect for difference.

How can we become more conscious of these co-creative aspects? How can we learn to tune into a climate of contribution and responsiveness?

We can't learn this skill, but there comes a point at which we can't prevent it from happening. I believe both contribution and responsiveness are natural tendencies in human beings. They are part of our creative urge. On our path to redefining our contribution, it is helpful also to develop our responsive side. Listening to ourselves has brought us this far, listening to others will take us further. Listening to the whole and to what wants to emerge might sound very abstract at first, but it can be learnt. As we develop a sense of the internal process that has led us to where we are now, we begin to sense processes around us with much more clarity. We begin to translate feelings and intuition into a different level of understanding reality. When we reflectively sense what is needed, the form of our contribution changes. We do not need to push things through anymore. We can test resonance, integrate responses and resiliently bring in our gifts. As we move from self-assertion to contribution and from self-sacrifice to responsiveness, we notice that we have an impact on the climate of interaction between ourselves and others. Not always, but sometimes, we will notice that people join in. We might be able to touch in others what is essentially human: a sense of collective creativity. We probably touch a longing that is as old as humankind. We hit the human capacity to lead together. Why *collective* leadership? Because leading for sustainability is not an act in isolation, neither is it a heroic contribution others willingly need to follow. It requires leadership by various individuals towards a similar goal on a collective scale, sometimes without knowing about one another, rarely with central coordination and always as a collective learning journey. It is also the acknowledgement that the capacity for leading, initiating, facilitating and sustaining the construction of meaningful futures is enfolded in all of us. Some take it up, others not; some are more skilled, others less so. But the inherent capacity resides in all of us. Collective leadership does not undervalue the wealth and power of individual ideas and vision, or the commitment and sustenance it requires to bring them to life. Rather, the notion of collective leadership adds to our individual leadership endeavour a significant insight. We know that our own vision is important, but is never entirely manifested and held by us alone. Our vision, then, is an expression of the myriad possibilities of consciousness and we happen to hold it. By the time we express it, it has undergone a process of its own emergence predicated on encounters and dialogues with many people. So although it is manifesting through us, it is not owned by us. We also know that the future is constantly emerging as a result of the 'space in between', a room of encounter between us and other people, a space released or blocked by communication. The more dialogic this space is allowed to be, the more likely that it leads to a state of sustainable co-creation. Collective leadership, then, is more than collaboratively doing things together as leaders or aiming at something ensuring collective input. It is taking on our leadership responsibility with a flexibility and awareness that is in line with what we sense is needed. We hold our leadership in an inner space of responsiveness and contribution to the common good with no need to excel or impose. We cultivate our capacity to see future possibilities and facilitate innovation and inventiveness. Our strength rests on our mindfulness because we have taken steps to access the whole of humanity in our own humanity first. As a result we become caring, compassionate and more deeply concerned with the collective good.

Mandy knew that redefining her leadership contribution would not necessarily mean a change in her profession, her focus of work or her client base. Whatever would emerge could gradually be integrated into her consultancy business. But the one aspect she decided to concentrate on more was the conscious creation of collective space between leaders because this was where she felt most at home and most herself:

> When I am in a place where there is collective leadership, there is almost an implicit awareness of the other's need; I wouldn't dream of thinking through something without

reference to the others, I am just speaking from experience, when I am in the space with others and we take something on in collective leadership, there is always this attentiveness to where the others are and no insistence that people move at your pace or follow where you are going ... you can suspend your own thinking.

If we attend to our own contribution as much as we show responsiveness to others and to the situation; we enter a space where collective intelligence can flow more easily. Solutions, agreements, strategies, and changes are often more sustainable when they are generated through diversity and engagement. The intelligence that can develop here does not rest on individual brilliance, but on a process of construction that requests diverse input. Collective intelligence does not undervalue individual intelligence; rather, the opposite is true. Processes aimed at collective intelligence make more effective use of individual intelligence. They ensure that nothing is lost and build on willingness to contribute and create. Decentralized software development, participatory dictionaries and large group change interventions are just a few examples where the use of collective intelligence furthers the common good. The coffee initiative, though never explicitly built on collective intelligence, developed its success through the continuous creation of shared space in which contributions could merge into agreeable outcomes.

When we search our memories we find our own experience of collective intelligence at work – be it in meetings where ideas are exchanged, the conversation builds on one another's contribution and it is fun to arrive at an unthinkable but exciting outcome; or a crisis situation in which those who are fighting suddenly join in to find a solution. But we might also remember the many situations where collective intelligence was not at work – the meeting in which nobody said what was really important, only to discuss the real issues afterwards with a close colleague; the workshop that was boring throughout with predictable results, the serial monologues of leaders who feel they need to stand their ground and compete. You probably remember even more examples.

When Lesley looked back at her leadership position in the multinational bank that made her feel more and more alienated from her heart and her passion for life, she recalled many situations in which collective intelligence was stifled:

> If you are in a meeting that is supposed to move efficiently towards a tangible outcome, and you feel your voice isn't being heard, that isn't really collective responsibility, it is just groupthink. It is not possible for you to say something different from anybody else. It is the story of 'The Emperor's New Clothes'. I can't say that the emperor has no clothes on, I say they are lovely. Not having the courage to say what I disagree with is somehow humiliating, but almost normal in the corporate world. I say what everybody says, because it takes particular courage to raise a voice that is different from everybody else in the room. In this company it felt much safer to rather say nothing in the meeting, and then say 'I am not standing up for that, I didn't agree with it' to close colleagues afterwards. This kind of communication does not take people's potential into account.

Looking back at memories of collective intelligence at work, you may realize that whenever it was present there was engagement, fun, and excitement. There was a drive to engage and overcome difficulties in a collective effort. Collective intelligence is greatly supported by forms of communicating and being with each other that engender respect, encourage people to speak from the heart, cultivate the art of listening and help people to be in the situation while observing their own thoughts, what is happening and how the process flows. As human beings we dwell in the house of language. That is why the way we communicate is so important. In speaking with each other, we create our internal worlds and so bring forth a world together. 'Doing dialogue' has been developing in the communication history of humankind for hundreds of years around the globe in different variations with essentially the same setting – allowing people to express their views in a structured way held by the goodwill and belief that collective intelligence can only emerge from variety and difference, and that the right thing to do, the *Truth* will always arise out of attentiveness and listening to difference. Dialogue derives strength from the diversity of opinions and insights that are brought into the circle. It thrives on contribution and responsiveness. Dialogic conversations are more likely to occur when we feel we can contribute authentically. This happens when the atmosphere feels safe, in the sense of non-judgement and respect for one another's internal worlds. The more fear and mistrust there is, the more people will resort to self-defense, judgement and withheld opinions.

When you begin to develop your redefined leadership contribution you may need courage to change the discourse of some of the conversational patterns in which you find yourself. It is worthwhile, though not easy, to speak more and more from the heart, say what you really mean, offer your observations respectfully and express what is important to you. In the end, this is what makes things move – that you do not withhold who you are. This does not mean that it will always work. But I encourage you not to be discouraged when you fail to find resonance. Sometimes the reason is that you lack courage or heart in your voice; sometimes it's simply because the people around you might not be able to hear the difference in voice. Do *not* give up. You may want to find a circle of people with whom you can converse in a different way. This can help establish your new voice. But be aware that the dialogic form of conversations needs to be brought back into ordinary life, ordinary business, and societal and global development. Sustainable leadership action hinges on our ability to have meaningful conversations and collective reflection. Dialogic conversations are a cornerstone of the global learning journey towards sustainability (see page 249).

In Ethiopia, Samson lives in a fragmented society where a high degree of compliance with the views of the government is vital for people's survival. And yet he believes in a dialogic approach to change:

> What has to be done is to take dialogic conversations into our organizations and then develop them into a structure that can respond to our complexities in the world. For example, a multinational corporation cannot really be run through circles of conversing people, but what you can learn from dialogue is that the best you can bring out in people is brought out in such circles of diversity. And this can be applied in organizations of all kind. If you create artificial compartmentalization you lose a lot of people's intelligence and abilities.

A Glimpse into Theory: Dialogue and Collective Creativity

Human intelligence must be seen both as an individual and a collective phenomenon. Dialogue is a communicative structure, and as such can become a container for the awareness of mutuality and interdependence, because in a circle hierarchy is not structurally exposed, nor are lines of communication influenced by the seating order. But the essence is that each person sees herself as as important as he or she sees the others, and therefore everybody respects a space in which each person's aspect or point of view is heard and valued. Through such a process the collective endeavour is nourished by diversity of mind and the same reality can be seen from as many angles as possible. Dialogue does not necessarily imply harmony, but respect for difference. The truth emerges not in competition or hierarchy, but in the form of a settling in of insight as a natural result of openness and variety of thought. It can be concluded by each individual. Facilitating this flow of mind's capacities and intelligence could lie at the core of sustainability leadership. This would be founded on the belief that the emergence of the collectively meaningful requires insight that only truly shared endeavours – in which diversity is seen as an asset – can bring about the changes towards sustainability the world so desperately needs (Berry, 1999; Elgin, 2001; Capra, 2003). In recent times, the idea of dialogue has been adopted far more for communication processes in the corporate world (Isaacs, 1999; Wheatley, 1999; Jaworsky, et al., 1996). Dialogue derives strength from the diversity of opinions and insights that are brought into the circle. However, dialogic settings are essentially human and have a long tradition in human history. An example is the *lekgotla*, a way of governance practised by traditional societies in the southern African region. It is a forum for open communication and decision-making with the participation of usually all adult members of a community (De Liefde, 2003). The aim is to come to a decision that is in line with the collective good and interest. Key to its success is an attitude of trust and respect for one another. Leadership must lead as an example of this. Each person attending has the right to express whatever she or he feels is important: 'Sharing the truth is at the heart of the *legkotla* system. There are no negative consequences for those involved. Fear of losing face is no longer an issue ... Participants experience that their opinions count and that they are actively involved in a communal quest for truth and meaning.' (De Liefde, 2003, p. 60).

The idea of dialogue has made its way into companies, international forums and sustainability initiatives. Stakeholder involvement has never been so high on the agenda (Isaacs, 1999; De Liefde, 2003). But not every communication that is called a dialogue really allows for communicative structures that enable collective intelligence to emerge. Bill Isaacs, in his book *Dialogue and the Art of Thinking Together,* has elaborated in a more Western rational approach the many ingredients necessary for leading through dialogue and collective intelligence. In his writings he emphasizes the need for leaders who want to lead through dialogue to develop their own awareness, about themselves, the space surrounding us and the diversity of others (Isaacs, 1999). His approach to dialogic conversations is grounded in the teachings of David Bohm. As a quantum scientist, Bohm has come to think about human communication in the form of dialogue through his insight into the wholeness of reality and the non-locality of different events in time that are all interconnected (Bohm, 1980). This led him to hope that a wider understanding of reality among humankind would enable people to communicate in a new way. This would require awareness of the mechanisms of fear, self-growth and mistrust that jeopardize human intelligence and harmony:

'It is clear if we are to live in harmony with ourselves and with nature we need to be able to communicate freely in a creative movement in which no one permanently holds to or otherwise defends his own ideas ... When we come

CHAPTER SIX: SUSTAINABILITY

together to talk, or otherwise to act in common, can each of us be aware of the subtle fears and pleasure sensations that block his ability to listen freely? Without this awareness, the injunction to listen to the whole of what is said will have little meaning. But if each one of us can give full attention to what is actually blocking communication while he is also attending properly to the content of what is communicated, then we may be able to create something new between us, something of very great significance for bringing to an end the at present insoluble problems of the individual and society.' (Bohm, 1996, p. 4 and p. 5).

When we see our redefined leadership contribution as a collective endeavour in a dialogic space, we realise that we are not the only ones struggling to map out the path towards sustainability. This does not free us from the responsibility to walk our path, but we know: we lead collectively. How we do this is important. The perception of leadership as an individual phenomenon is only a surface perception. Our traditional focus on individual leadership may blind us to understanding the complex dynamics that underlie the surface reality that shows powerful and influential leaders.

Lucia has moved to a new job in the corporate centre of the multinational company. Coming from a more decentralized department gave her insight into a structural pattern that she had not been fully aware of:

> It is fascinating working in the corporate centre now, which I never have done before. You see that pathology of self-serving being acted out. We have people who sit on the top floor, the CEO and his executives. And the whole building is in service to these people. It is not in service to the business or the rest of the organization, or the global society, it isn't. I can

really see what that means, because you are in service to the personalities and not necessarily the collective good.

She noticed that the implicit leadership model is furthering hierarchical layers of individual heroic leaders. The future of the organization seemed to be set in a pattern of push and pull between the self-assertion of certain people and the submission and compliance of others. Lucia observed how this pattern of co-creation trickled down, affecting every layer of the organization, a culture that was very difficult to change.

We may ask ourselves more truthfully if the dynamics we see and the dynamics we ourselves cause are fragmenting forms of co-creation or sustainable patterns of co-creation. The answer is not important – *what is important is to recognize co-creative patterns that are life-enhancing.* We can learn from these. This is what we need more of. Life-enhancing patterns of co-creation might be more time-consuming in the beginning. They call for more complex approaches to change. But in the end, this might lead to a more sustainable situation, a vital equilibrium at the edge of chaos. Only when we cease to communicate and learn is the system likely to fall off the edge. Sustainable action needs an inner willingness to learn 'at the edge of chaos', ideally in a state of equilibrium between stability and instability. Whenever we contribute to the wholeness of a situation, to that of a process, to our own wholeness and that of others, we foster the emergence of life-enhancing patterns of co-creation.

How can we contribute to wholeness more consciously?

We need to complement our outward leadership for sustainability with our own internal change and start with ourselves. If we remain fragmented and disintegrated as we walk through life, we will create the same outside of us. Reconnecting with our quest and the initial intention strengthens the thread of our leadership journey and it contributes to our own wholeness. The more bal-

CHAPTER SIX: SUSTAINABILITY

anced and, at the same time, flexible our identity becomes, the less energy we need to spend on self-defense and the more we will be able to contribute according to what we sense is needed to create wholeness. We become one centre that supports other centres. We enter the complexity of mutually reinforcing support and through this, contribute to wholeness. We can feel the wholeness as it reflects back to us – it is a feeling of comfort and gratitude. We can feel the arousal of the heart. This has a healing effect on us, because it makes us feel more human. As we contribute more and more to wholeness it makes us feel more alive.

Knowing that the expansion of our own wholeness and humanity is a pathway to sustainable leadership action, we can look at our own leadership patterns with the intention of becoming more flexible in our contribution. Based on our particular journey we all feel more or less comfortable in a certain way of leading. It helps to become aware of our patterns and preferences. Thus we can overcome our habits and boundaries and expand the choices we have in leading. The observation of our preferences and the expansion of our possibilities can be greatly supported by a leadership model that is based on archetypal leadership energies. All of them bring forth a certain aspect of contributing to the whole, yet, in their togetherness, they can shift a situation towards healing and collective intelligence. We may recognize which energy we are used to cultivating and displaying and which we have alienated ourselves from. This can be a step towards deeper integration when we gradually unleash our potential so that we can embrace all the energies as and when they are needed in order to provide what is missing in any given situation. The archetypal energies we may look into are the energy of the lover, the warrior and the magician (see page 250).

We have a preference for *sovereign energy* when we are used to leading up front with a strong voice and the expectation that we know the right path. In our fully developed sovereign energy we feel connected with our centre. Mythologically, the sovereign speaks on behalf of 'the whole', but in fact, the whole is speaking through him/her. Characteristic of sovereign energy is centeredness and calmness, the capacity to decide, as well as organizing and creative power, structuredness and an attitude of service. Ideally we live what we expect from others. In our leadership we are firmly behind a goal we believe in. We are prepared to inspire others to join us. From sovereign energy we see in other people their value and potential without needing perfection – we want to contribute to them making use of their potential. The trust we have in ourselves stems from a trust in life, and the knowing that what we follow is a purpose in service of life, a purpose that goes beyond our individuality. Our integrity and authenticity are visible, we have a clear mission and we speak from the heart. We take initiative not from self-interest, but in the interests of all. Progress inspires us. We are convinced that the whole is best served through giving direction and inspiration.

When we lack sovereign energy we find it difficult to believe in our path. Our voice may be weak and we withhold what we really need to say or do. We lack trust in our abilities to contribute, we doubt our initiative and find it difficult to act purposefully. We gladly delegate the upfront leading to other people.

If we overemphasize our sovereign energy, we might be in danger of moving into our shadow side. This happens under stress or when we lose the connection to the whole and our deeper self. The most obvious symptom is that we ignore participation and feedback. If things get worse, we become narcissistic and suffer from vanity. As the imbalance progresses, ignorance of our own weakness grows and we become dominant, dictatorial, abusive or simply tyrannical. We sustain our power by all means, and do not allow the slightest criticism. Cruelty is the logical consequence. As a shadow sovereign we impose our law on others.

CHAPTER SIX: SUSTAINABILITY

When we want to develop a balanced sovereign energy it is helpful to ask the following questions:

What is the greater interest here (the interest of the whole)?
How can I inspire others?
Am I living what I expect others to be?
How can I be of service here?
Do I speak from the heart?
What is my contribution here?
Do I invite feedback?
Do I help others to develop who they are?

When we have a preference for the *lover energy* we like to create connection above everything else. We deeply know and feel that all is one, all is interconnected and interdependent. We sense that boundaries are permeable and separate identities are just different manifestations of the great life force that binds everything together. When we lead with lover energy we take care of others and try to enhance their life force, their beauty and their inner strength. We know empathy and often act out of intuition. We ensure inclusion and participation and do not rest before we are assured that all voices are heard. We cultivate the art of relating to others. Our prime mode is giving and we pour out compassion from a never-ending source. We are passionate about our purposeful action, and love beauty and the arts. We feel connected to the creative force of life, and foster innovation. In the lover energy our prevailing state of mind is gratitude; we can see the beauty in life's details, a smile in the street, a beautiful landscape, a child playing, a blossoming flower, an encounter with another human being. We are convinced that the whole is best served through inclusion and community-building.

When we lack lover energy we feel cut off from our centre, from the creative life force and from our emotions. We hardly express what we feel. We become depressed and forget what life is all about, or we neglect all personal aspects including our own. We are constantly driven and do not consider relationship building very important.

When our lover energy becomes disconnected from our centre we feel dependent on other people's approval, their attention, and thrive only where we are emotionally supported. We can become restless in the search for a feeling of an ultimate unity that cannot exist in the material, the physical world. We avoid conflicts and want to create harmony at all costs. We develop a tendency towards possessiveness, looking for nourishing life energy through encounters with other people only. As the imbalance progresses we become addicted to people or substances.

When we want to develop balanced lover energy it is helpful to ask the following questions:

>How do other people feel about this?
>How am I part of creating this situation?
>Am I taking care of my boundaries?
>Who needs to be included?
>Have I listened carefully?
>How can I step aside and observe rather than be overwhelmed by my feelings?

When we have a preference for *warrior energy* we admire mastery and professional clarity. We believe in discipline and hard work. Our centeredness is based on skilfulness and concentration. We happily serve a purpose that requires us to use all our strength and capability. What we do we do with courage and determination, and believe that obstacles are to be overcome. We know how to assert our boundaries and are willing to fight for a goal we can happily serve and align with. When we fight, it is for a purpose

CHAPTER SIX: SUSTAINABILITY

beyond our individual self and in the interest of a larger goal we believe in. We are inspired by change for the better, even at the risk of our own life. Our invulnerability stems from our inner source of clarity and alertness. What we do, we do thoroughly. When we know what to fight for we feel the vitality of life, with respect for both fellow warriors and enemies. Our prime mode is action and quick decisions, and we avoid doubt and hesitation. We sometimes see reflection as a waste of time. Honesty, ethics and truthfulness guide us. We usually have analytical skills and can cut to the core of the matter. We are not afraid of conflicts, if they are necessary in achieving our goal. Our limits are those we set and we experience difficulties as challenges. We believe that the whole is best served by performance, mastery and determination.

When we lack warrior energy we find it difficult to handle confrontations and steer through crises. We have difficulty committing to anything and lack determination because we are not sure about the goal. We hesitate because there are too many aspects to consider. We easily give in and often let other people walk over our boundaries. We lose access to our vital energy and feel like a victim or a wounded warrior.

When we overemphasize warrior energy we begin to enjoy fighting for the sake of fighting. It becomes a habit. We might get attached to the feeling of victories and the thrill of warrior mode. We can lose ourselves in the pursuit of a false goal, or fighting on behalf of people who did not mandate us to do so. We dismiss people who do not display the same warrior energy and do not accept them as equals. We concentrate on performance only and are in danger of moving into burnout. When we lose our centre every move around us becomes a potential attack and we may become violent. We build armour around us, and display no emotions.

When we want to develop balanced warrior energy it is helpful to ask the following questions:

CHAPTER SIX: SUSTAINABILITY

What am I fighting for? Is it worth it and for whom?
How can I find centeredness?
What is my mission and how is it aligned with other people's mission?
Do I respect others and do I respect people who are different from me?
What is my practice of mastery and mindfulness?
What do we need beyond performance?

When we have a preference for *magician energy* we have a good sense of the whole as well as its parts and are skilful in navigating between the two. We know how to connect the individual with the larger issue, and this is why we invite and integrate a variety of perspectives. We like to lead from behind, and often through facilitation. The magician knows that there is more to reality than what can be seen on the surface. We are like a shaman or a healer who is prepared to connect the surface level of reality with a deeper level. This understanding of the connection between the invisible and the visible world enables us to access meaning and purpose on a deeper level. We can help people make sense of their tasks and their path. We are aware of processes and the link between process and outcome. We can guide through detached involvement, through our capacity to gain perspective in the middle of a storm. We see interdependencies, rhythm and relatedness other people don't easily notice. We can shift outcomes by changing the discourse in conversations, because we ask questions that resonate with people's souls and offer insights that would otherwise be lost. Ideally, we can help people be more at ease and feel safe in the world. This leads to trust in the collective endeavour. The magician is an interpreter of reality and this transforms reality in a powerful way. In our presence people feel they can say what needs to be said. We enjoy change because we know it is a faithful companion throughout life. Our prime mode is observation and thoughtfulness. We believe

CHAPTER SIX: SUSTAINABILITY

we best contribute to the whole through perspective, integration of difference and reflection.

When we lack magician energy, we have a disdain for processes and usually ignore other layers of reality. We find having to deal with difference a block to progress and experience reflection as uncomfortable. We tend to be convinced of our standpoint and we judge other opinions negatively.

When we overemphasize magician energy, we feel we know much more than others and we use the power of knowing the different layers of reality to manipulate others or to enhance our own power. We lead by intrigue. Our detachment deteriorates into emotional distance. If the imbalance grows, we assume a secret superiority and exert influence through skilful manipulation. We cultivate our own omnipotence.

When we want to develop balanced magician energy it is helpful to ask the following questions:

Do my insights really serve?
What is the role of my ego in this?
What are the different layers of reality here?
How can I acknowledge difference?
How can I bring in different perspectives?
What is needed to access a sense of meaning?
How can I change the discourse?
What pattern can I observe?

By now you may have recognized what your preferences are and what feels alien to you. Or you might have thought of other people who resembled one or other of the energies. It is important not to judge yourself or other people according to what their preferences are, but to notice how these different energies can all be enacted in favour of the collective good. Leadership for sustainability needs all four archetypal energies. In their ideal form they all contribute to wholeness, but the key is that they do so most in their togetherness. We need all of them to lead towards a more sustainable future: direction, inspiration, inclusion, community building, performance, mastery, determination, perspective, integration of difference, reflection. A one-sided approach will not succeed.

I would like to encourage you to begin observing the impact of your preferences and what you tend to neglect. Then begin to observe how these different energies are enacted in your leadership environment. What is missing? What is overemphasized? What is the impact of this?

Gradually you can map your own path towards more integrated leadership through developing the parts you have been neglecting so far, or rebalancing what you have overemphasized. Be patient with your ability to change habits, while opening yourself to deeper integration. Your redefined leadership contribution is more likely to find resonance when you have expanded your choices of leading. This enables you to contribute to wholeness more consciously – in your personal life, in a particular situation, in an organization you are leading or in a process you have initiated. This also enables you to see the different energies on a larger scale. When you begin to observe your own corporate world, change processes, societal setups and sustainability initiative, then you can begin to observe which energies are taken care of and which are missing. You may notice that sustainable progress is more likely to occur when the different energies become balanced over time. With your own growing ability to enact the different leadership energies as and when they are required you can accelerate this progress. You will notice that at times another person provides what is missing because he or she feels more comfortable in this quality of leadership energy. Observe its impact and acknowledge it. There is an intuitive human capacity to create wholeness. The more conscious we are, however, the more we help our world.

CHAPTER SIX: SUSTAINABILITY

When you are in a process of redefining your leadership contribution towards a more sustainable world, remember that these ingredients belong in the recipe for creating wholeness:

- Your state of mind and your willingness to act towards growing sustainability in the world counts. Your commitment and faithful intent will have an influence on the path in front of you. You can make a difference.
- There is never only one solution to a problem or a necessary innovation – your ability to nurture diversity in yourself and around you is the ground for sustainable solutions. The whole is best enacted through participation and partnership. A constant flow between acknowledgement of difference and integrating it is the basic rhythm of life.
- The global learning journey towards sustainability needs circles of reflection and dialogic communication patterns, on a small scale and on a large scale. Learning to observe what we do while we do it is a competence that will be needed more and more in the future. This is the best way to ensure that collective intelligence can flow freely. Your willingness to enter this dialogic space is an important contribution.
- Leading towards sustainability requires collective leadership. Your ability to do what needs doing collectively in flexible leadership roles eases progress. Community-building is important for any sustainable leadership action because many people are needed to do what needs doing – and they will only do it if they have a sense of belonging to the future.

Now that you have almost finished this book, your flight might be over, your holiday almost finished or your routine demanding that you put the book aside. You might just have begun to acknowledge that there is a deeper quest that you have long neglected, or you may be about to move into what you have identified as your new leadership path. Wherever you are I encourage you to stay faithful to your journey. Once upon a time your heart knew, and your mind listened. Give them a chance to remarry.

There is nothing more beautiful than the recognition and acknowledgement of each other's humanness. Where humanity sees itself in another, there is the deepest hope and potential for human development and the taking care of possibilities entrusted to the human race. Wherever this is missing there is an inherent tendency that violence and ignorance will prevail. The acknowledgment of your own humanness precedes the deep respect for others. If there is one thing I would recommend, it would be: stay connected with the quest that originated in your deeper initial intention. Sustainability needs us as whole as possible. It needs the reunion of mind and heart. The world needs your refined leadership contribution.

When I lived and worked in Zimbabwe for five years, before the country was ruled into chaos and difference in opinion was brutally suppressed, I often listened to the songs of Oliver Mutukudzi. He was a hero symbol for Zimbabweans of all ages as he not only portrayed the sense of pride and freedom the independence of the country had given people, but was also at times critical of the new government. One day he gave a concert in the small town I was living in, organized by a friend of mine. As is a most loved tradition in Zimbabwe, Oliver encouraged people to come up and dance on the stage. It would have been very impolite to refuse and so I found myself dancing on the stage. This was quite far beyond my comfort zone so I remember the scene very well. The song he sang was about a little boy visiting his grandfather and saying to him: 'Are you very old, Grandpa?' In Africa, old age always stands for wisdom. And the Grandpa says: 'Yes, very, very old', and he laughed. Then the boy says: 'Tell me what you know!' And the Grandpa says: 'If you have a word, say it out loud, say it from the heart; and if you have a song, sing it out loud, sing it from the heart!'

CHAPTER SIX: SUSTAINABILITY

Reflections:

What is your pattern of self-protection — do you tend to assert yourself or withhold your contribution? No matter the situation, what is your tendency?

What are the archetypal energies you have cultivated most? Which of them would you like to develop more?

If you were free to choose, what would be the contribution you would most like to make to a more sustainable world?

If you had to describe your quest in a few sentences how would it sound?

What are the next steps on your leadership journey?

Chapter 6: Summary:

- When our latent desire to make a difference is touched we long for more. Meaning is the most nourishing life force. If it touches us we are drawn to it, not without doubts, but with progressive commitment.
- Sustainable action is an individual, organizational, societal and global learning process. We can become more conscious partners of evolution. Nourishing our deeper intention helps us to align our outer journey with our inner potential so that we can humbly join a global learning process.
- The journey to sustainability cannot be delegated to a few people. It is everybody's business, so it is our business. It calls for action and it calls for circles of reflection and dialogue. Only collectively can we find the most suitable path. We need to create a network of mutually supportive centres.
- The voice of our heart is important. We learn to trust it more as we reach out to our own humanity. Then we no longer need to indulge in the many rituals of self-defense. Forgetfulness of self is a gift we receive on the journey; mindfulness is the gift we give back to the world.
- A dynamic balance of responsiveness and contribution allows for a more sustainable generative pattern of co-creation. Both contribution and responsiveness are natural tendencies in human beings. Human future is emerging as a result of a 'space in between', an encounter between people. The more dialogic this space is the more likely it is that it will lead to sustainable patterns of co-creation.
- Leading for sustainability requires collective leadership: the ability to do what needs doing and the flexibility to take on leadership as required. This works best when we recognize patterns of co-creation that are life-enhancing. These we need to develop further.

BIBLIOGRAPHY

Alexander, Christopher, 2002: *The Nature of Order – Book One, The Phenomenon of Life*, Centre for Environmental Studies, Berkeley, California

Bateson, Gregory, 2000: *Steps to an Ecology of Mind*, The University of Chicago Press, Chicago and London

Berry, Thomas, 1999: *The Great Work*, Bell Tower, New York

Bohm, David, 1980: *Wholeness and the Implicate Order*, Routledge, London and New York

Bohm, David, 1996: *On Dialogue*, edited by Lee Nichels, Routledge, London and New York

Brennon, Ann, 1988: *Hands of Light,* Bantam Books, New York

Buber, Martin, 1962: *Das Dialogische Prinzip*, Lambert Schneider, Gelingen, Germany

Buber, Martin, 1970: *I and Thou*, Touchstone, Simon and Schuster, New York

Capra, Fritjof, 1996: *The Web of Life*, Anchor Books, New York

Capra, Fritjof, 2003: *The Hidden Connection*, A Science for Sustainable Living, Flamingo Press, London

Choucri, Nazli, 1996: Quote taken from http://www.cdnarchitect.com/asf/perspectives_sustainibility

De Liefde, H. J. Willem, 2003: *Lekgotla, The Art of Leadership Through Dialogue*, Jacana, Houghton, South Africa

Elgin, Duane, 2000: Promise Ahead, *A Vision of Hope and Action For Humanity's Future*, 2000, Harper Collins, New York

Fleischmann, Paul R., 1999: *Karma and Chaos*, Vipassana Research Publications, Seattle

Greenleaf, Robert K., 1977: *Servant Leadership, A Journey Into The Nature Of Legitimate Power And Greatness*, Paulist Press, New York

Helgesen, Sally, 1995: *The Web of Inclusion*, Doubleday, New York

Isaacs, William, 1999: *Dialogue and The Art Of Thinking Together*, A pioneering Approach to Communicating in Business and in Life, Currency Doubleday

Jaworski, Joseph, 1996: *Synchronicity – The Inner Path Of Leadership*, Berrett Koehler, San Francisco

Jones, Micheal, 2000: *Leading Living Organizations-, learning to think as Nature Thinks*, unpublished paper, www.pianoscapes.com

Kauffman, Stuart, 1993: *The Origin of Order*, Oxford University Press, New York

Kauffman, Stuart, 1995: *At Home In The Universe, The Search for The Laws of Self-Organization and Complexity*, Oxford University Press, New York, Oxford

Krishnamurti, J., 1978: *The Wholeness of Life*, Krishnamurti Foundation India, Madras

Krishnamurti J.; Bohm, David, 1985: *The Ending of Time*, Krishnamurti Foundation Hampshire, England

Krishnamurti, J.; Bohm, David, 1986: *The Future Of Humanity*, Krishnamurti Foundation, Madras, India

Macy, Joanna, 1991a: *The Dharma of Natural Systems – Mutual Causality in Buddhism and General Systems Theory*, State University of New York Press, New York

Macy, Joanna, 1991b: *World as Lover, World As Self*, Parallax Press., Berkeley, California

Maturana, Humberto and Veraly, Francisco, J., 1987: *The Tree of Knowledge: The Biological Roots of Human Understanding*, Shambhala, Boston

Prigogine, Ilya, 1996: *The End Of Certainty, Time Chaos and The New Laws of Nature*, The Free Press, New York

Prigogine, Ilya, and Stengers, Isabelle, 1984: *Order out of Chaos*. New York, London, etc: Bantam Books

Rahula, Walpola, 1959: *What The Buddha Taught*, The Gordon Fraser Gallery Ltd., London and Bedford

Sahtouris, Elisabeth, James E. Lovelock, 2000: *Earthdance, Living Systems in Evolution*, iUniversity Press, San Jose, New York, Lincoln, Shanghai

Scharmer, Claus Otto, 2000: *Presencing: Learning From the Future As It Emerges*, Paper presented at the Conference on Knowledge and Innovation, May 25-26 2000, Helsinki School of Economics, Finnland

Scharmer, Claus Otto, 2007: *Theory U: Leading from the Future as it Emerges*, SoL, The Society for Organizational Learning, Boston

Varela J. Francisco, 1999: *Ethical Know-How-Action, Wisdom and Cognition*, Stanford University Press, Stanford

Varela, J. Francisco; Thompson, Evan; and Rosch, Eleanor, 1991: *The Embodied Mind: Cognitive Science and Human Experience*, MIT Press, Cambridge MA

Wheatley, Margaret, 1999: *Leadership and The New Science, Discovering Order In A Chaotic World*, Berrett-Koehler Publishers, San Francisco

Wiener, Norbert, 1967: *Human Use of Human Beings, Cybernetics and Society*, New York, Avon Books

World Commission on Environment and Development (WCED), 1987: *Our Common Future, Report of the World Commission on Environment and Development*, Oxford University Press, New York

Zohar, Dana, Marshall, Ian, 1994: *The Quantum Society, Mind Physics and A New Social Vision*, Quill, William Morrow, New York

THE CYCLE OF TRANSITION

Profound reflection

- Reflective and generative stability
- Openness to new possibilities and willingness to contribute
- Feeling comfortable in the unknown

- Reflective instability
- Reorganization of memory
- Preparedness to venture into the unknown

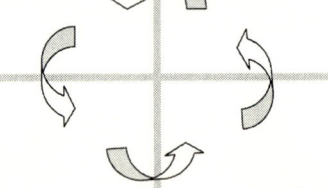

Order   *Chaos*

- Unreflective, maintained stability
- Confirmation of memory
- Knowing how things are

- Unreflective instability, internal chaos
- Disintegration of the familiar
- Feeling of dissatisfaction with oneself and the world.

No profound reflection

See page 124   Source: Otto Scharmer, 2000, adapted by Petra Kuenkel

GENERATIVE ENERGIES

Passion

Inspiration
Creativity
Arousal of the Heart

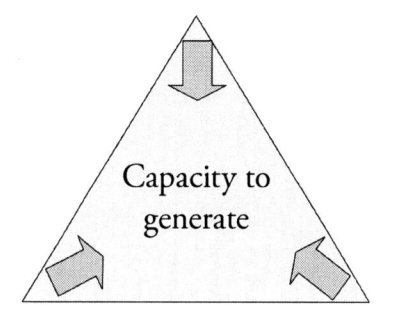

Capacity to generate

Commitment

Perseverance
Endurance

Contemplation

Reflection
Stillness
Meditation

See page 151   Source: Petra Kuenkel, based on conversations with Robert Cran

CO-CREATION

collective co-creation
leading towards sustainability

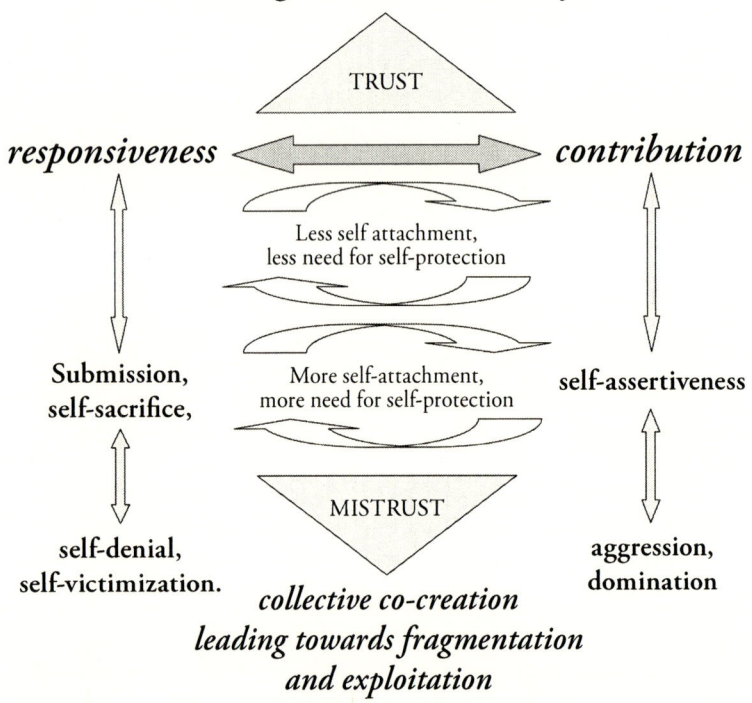

TRUST

responsiveness ⇔ *contribution*

Less self attachment,
less need for self-protection

More self-attachment,
more need for self-protection

Submission,
self-sacrifice,

self-assertiveness

MISTRUST

self-denial,
self-victimization.

aggression,
domination

collective co-creation
leading towards fragmentation
and exploitation

See page 218   Source: Petra Kuenkel, based on conversations with Robert Cran

DIALOGIC CONVERSATIONS

Voicing

Speaking from a deeper level of the self, speaking from the heart, having the feeling that something needs to be said

Suspending

Holding sufficiently lightly what I think is certain Acknowledge and observe thoughts and opinions without identifying with it (I am not my opinion)

Emergence of collective intelligence

Listening

Listening from the heart, listening as if one knew that what is "out there" in the other person, is also in here, in me to partake of and take part in

Respecting

Awareness of the integrity of another person and reaching out to understand it, trying to understand how everything fits

See page 226

Source: Bill Isaacs, Peter Garrett

ARCHETYPAL LEADERSHIP ENERGIES

Sovereign energy

Taking initiative
*Being inspired by the idea that will work
Speaking on behalf of the whole*
self-confidence and trust in others

Magician

Ensuring perspective
*Holding differences and
the process*

Stepping back to observe
Ability to create safety
Multi-level insight
Involved detachment

Emergence of collective leadership

Lover energy

Feeling empathy
*Experiencing it from the
other's point of view,
Taking care of the other*

Surrender to intuition
Patience
Ability to nurture

Warrior

Challenging respectfully
*Following a mission towards
a larger goal*

Clarity of boundaries
Willingness to perform
Decisiveness and determination

See page 231

Source: Cliff Barry, adapted by Bill Isaacs and Peter Garrett, adapted by Petra Kuenkel

Collective Leadership Institute
Building competence for sustainability

The *Collective Leadership Institute* is an independent non-profit organization based in Berlin, Germany, and Cape Town, South Africa. Its mission is to build dialogic process competence in sustainability engagement.

WE BELIEVE
that every private sector company, every public institution and every other organisation can be operated in a responsible and future-oriented way. The commitment to sustainability in its human, environmental, social and economic dimensions can become an integral part of business and societal development.

WE KNOW
from experience that sustainability engagement requires competence in dialogue, cooperation management and stakeholder involvement and that it calls for creative innovation and awareness about global interdependence.

WITH OUR
educational programs, project management and process-oriented research we build competence in collaborative sustainability engagement for leaders, project managers and change agents from corporations, small and medium sized companies, development agencies, the public sector and civil society organisations.

www.collectiveleadership.com

Printed in the United Kingdom
by Lightning Source UK Ltd.
131977UK00001B/29/P